The Three Musketeers—Le Panteau!

A pantomime

Richard Lloyd

Samuel French — London

© 2001 BY RICHARD LLOYD

Rights of Performance by Amateurs are controlled by Samuel French Ltd, 52 Fitzroy Street, London W1T 5JR, and they, or their authorized agents, issue licences to amateurs on payment of a fee. **It is an infringement of the Copyright to give any performance or public reading of the play before the fee has been paid and the licence issued.**

The Royalty Fee indicated below is subject to contract and subject to variation at the sole discretion of Samuel French Ltd.

        Basic fee for each and every
        performance by amateurs   Code K
        in the British Isles

The publication of this play does not imply that it is necessarily available for performance by amateurs or professionals, either in the British Isles or Overseas. Amateurs and professionals considering a production are strongly advised in their own interests to apply to the appropriate agents for written consent before starting rehearsals or booking a theatre or hall.

ISBN 0 573 16416 9

Please see page iv for further copyright information

THE THREE MUSKETEERS—LE PANTEAU!

First performed by the Theatre Workshop, Coulsdon, on Saturday, 9th December 2000, with the following cast:

Cardinal Richeleeugh	Richard Lloyd
Le Chevalier Du Lobster Roquefort	Steve North
Pus-sac	Jonathan Wales
D'Artagnan	Vanessa Hammick
Porthos	Rosie Martin
Aramis	Tanya Allison
Athos	Tina Poole
King Louis XXVLIIXVLIIIXXXVIII	Tim Young
Malady De Splinter	Lisa Lloyd
Queen Anne	Amy Coates
The Duke of Tottenham	Neil Grew
Monsieur De Trivialle	Penny Payne
Dame Desirée D'Artagnan	Chris Argles
Constant Hoh-hi-hon	Emma Rose
Zoot A Lor	Simon Crouch
Zach Rebleur	Heidi Bush
Plonquer	Peter Bird
Monsieur Hoh-hi-hon	David Cole
Tavern Wench	Kimberley Argles
Maurice	Mike Brown
Mother Inferior	Julia Swale
Gérard Drippy-Dew	Julie Wilson
Brother Bastinado	Mike Brown
Brother Strappado	Luke Argles
Cardinal's Guard	Paul Breden
	Chris Blakeney
	Chris Strachan
	Julie Wilson

Directed by **Richard Lloyd**
Musical Director, **Mark Taylor**
Technical Director, **Simon Poole**

© 2001 BY RICHARD LLOYD

Rights of Performance by Amateurs are controlled by Samuel French Ltd, 52 Fitzroy Street, London W1T 5JR, and they, or their authorized agents, issue licences to amateurs on payment of a fee. **It is an infringement of the Copyright to give any performance or public reading of the play before the fee has been paid and the licence issued.**

The Royalty Fee indicated below is subject to contract and subject to variation at the sole discretion of Samuel French Ltd.

       Basic fee for each and every
           performance by amateurs   Code K
           in the British Isles

The publication of this play does not imply that it is necessarily available for performance by amateurs or professionals, either in the British Isles or Overseas. Amateurs and professionals considering a production are strongly advised in their own interests to apply to the appropriate agents for written consent before starting rehearsals or booking a theatre or hall.

ISBN 978 0 573 16416 3

Please see page iv for further copyright information

CHARACTERS

Les Malfaisants:
Cardinal Richeleeugh, villainy incarnate
Malady De Splinter, a wicked lady
Le Chevalier Du Lobster Roquefort, debauched aristo, and agent of the evil Cardinal
Capitan Pus-sac, Commandante of the feared Cardinal's Guard
Les Garçons Principal:
D'Artagnan, un garçon principal impudent!
Porthos, un garçon principal gastronomique
Aramis, un garçon principal poétique
Athos, un garçon principal paralytique
La Grande Dame Pantomimique:
Dame Desirée D'Artagnan, la tante D'Artagnan
La Fille Principal:
Constant Hoh-hi-hon, une sex-kitten hapless
Les Hommes de Bon Virtue:
King Louis XXVLIIXVLIIIXXXVIII, by the grace of God, King of France
Queen Anne, une airhead royalismé
The Duke of Tottenham (Hotspur), Prime Minister D'Angleterre et all-round stud muffin … handsome but dim
Monsieur De Trivialle, Commandante of the King's Musketeers
Les Hommes Brokeurs:
Zoot A Lor & Zach Rebleur, of the Cardinal's Guard
Les Fromages:
Plonquer, un thief; Servant to D'Artagnan
Monsieur Hoh-hi-hon, un vielle geezer loopy! Purveyor of snails to the Court of Versailles
Mother Inferior, she has a dirty habit…
Les Animaux Pantomimique:
Gérard Drippy-Dew, un escargot pantomimique
Le Scuttle, a pantomime spider and glove puppet
L'Inquisition Sacré:
Brother Bastinado & Brother Strappado, Inquisitors Génerale

Plus dancing chorus of Cardinal's Guards, a few extra Musketeers, wenches, innkeepers, and so on

LES CHANSONS

1. Solo — D'Artagnan
2. Villains' duet — Richeleeugh & Roquefort
3. Ensemble — D'Artagnan and the Three Musketeers
4. Ensemble — D'Artagnan, Plonquer and the Three Musketeers
5. Audience Participation — Dame, Zoot and Zach
6. Romantic duet — D'Artagnan and Constant
7. Ensemble — D'Artagnan, Constant, Dame, Plonquer, and the Three Musketeers
8. Ensemble — The Company—barring baddies
9. Finale — The Company

SYNOPSIS OF SCENES

ACT I

Scene 1	Paris. The throne room of the Palais de Justice
Scene 2	Paris. A boulevard
Scene 3	A farmyard in Gascony
Scene 4	A wayside inn without Paris
Scene 5	Paris. The throne room of the Palais de Justice
Scene 6	A street without the Headquarters of the King's Musketeers
Scene 7	Paris. A street
Scene 8	The Tavern Contretemps in St Germain
Scene 9	The King's audience chamber in the Palais de Louvre
Scene 10	Elsewhere in the Palais de Louvre—the boudoir of Queen Anne
Scene 11	The courtyard of Monsieur Hoh-hi-hon

Entr'Acte

ACT II

Scene 1	The dungeon of the Bastille Prison
Scene 2	Paris. The throne room of the Palais de Justice
Scene 3	The banks of the Seine
Scene 4	The house of Monsieur Hoh-hi-hon
Scene 5	The King's audience chamber in the Palais de Louvre
Scene 6	Elsewhere in the Palais de Louvre—the boudoir of Queen Anne
Scene 7	The dungeon of the Bastille Prison
Scene 8	The King's audience chamber in the Palais de Louvre
Scene 9	Whitehall—the bedchamber of the Duke of Tottenham
Scene 10	Paris—a street
Scene 11	The Carmelite Convent at Bèthune, without then within
Scene 12	The house of Monsieur Hoh-hi-hon
Scene 13	The ballroom, the Palais de Versailles

The notice printed below on behalf of the Performing Right Society should be carefully read if any copyright music is used in this pantomime.

The permission of the owner of the performing rights in copyright music must be obtained before any public performance may be given, whether in conjunction with a play or sketch or otherwise, and this permission is just as necessary for amateur performances as for professional. The majority of copyright musical works (other than oratorios, musical plays and similar dramatico-musical works) are controlled in the British Commonwealth by the PERFORMING RIGHT SOCIETY LTD, 29-33 Berners Street, London W1P 4AA.

The Society's practice is to issue licences authorizing the use of its repertoire to the proprietors of premises at which music is publicly performed, or, alternatively, to the organizers of musical entertainments, but the Society does not require payment of fees by performers as such. Producers or promoters of plays, sketches, etc., at which music is to be performed, during or after the play or sketch, should ascertain whether the premises at which their performances are to be given are covered by a licence issued by the Society, and if they are not, should make application to the Society for particulars as to the fee payable.

A separate and additional licence from PHONOGRAPHIC PERFORMANCES LTD, 1 Upper James Street, London W1R 3HG, is needed whenever commercial recordings are used.

INTRODUCTION

I was keen to follow up my pantomime pastiche of *Treasure Island* with a panto makeover of another classic tale of derring-do.

And if *Treasure Island* is *the* definitive children's adventure story, then *The Three Musketeers* must count as a leading contender in the second rank.

Like *Treasure Island*, the appeal of *The Three Musketeers* seems to transcend ages and generations. And like *Treasure Island*, the story of *The Three Musketeers* seems to have made that rare transition where fiction slips quietly across the borders of literature, and into the enchanted realm of folklore. In truth, there have been so many adaptations of *The Three Musketeers* (and thus we all think we know the story so well) that few people could say for sure where the novel ends and fable begins.

To appreciate how fully this story has permeated the collective consciousness, consider how the very phrase "The Three Musketeers" has become a byword for any close-knit group of friends. Or how "All For One and One For All!" has passed into general usage as possibly the most famous rallying cry in the history of human literature.

This pantomime then, is a spoof of a distillation. It isn't based on the original novel, but on the story and characters which have become ingrained through endless film and TV adaptations, children's storybooks, and so on. As a result, our pastiche bears only a passing resemblance to M. Dumas's lengthy original. Mind you, the same could be said of most of the film adaptations!

Of course, as panto, no-one will expect *Le Panteau!* to stick too closely to the book... For one thing, D'Artagnan and the three Musketeers are envisaged as a quartet of Principal Boys.

Now in amateur theatre societies, actresses invariably outnumber actors by two or three to one—and yet most pantomimes provide for only two or three female principals. Well, this show boasts seven, and the avowed intention was to give the ladies a fair crack of the whip, and an opportunity to prove that they can roister and swashbuckle with the best of them!

On the subject of roistering, as far as good taste and discretion go, this script attempts to steer that ever tricky course between trying to satisfy the festive appetites of both adults and children. I'm afraid I don't subscribe to the theory that panto is purely for kids—a true pantomime should have plenty for everyone—and a proportion of the jokes in the present script are certainly aimed at the grown-ups. I can quite believe that one or two of these may prove slightly too near the knuckle for the taste of some societies. Should this be the case, any producer should of course feel free to omit or emend any quips which he or she may feel inappropriate for their particular audience. Each to their own...

Richard Lloyd

PRODUCTION NOTES

These notes are offered as helpful background to potential directors, and are not intended as prescriptive, or as a definitive guide. There is plenty of opportunity for individual interpretation in the staging of this show, and the author urges all societies to do their own thing with it, to their hearts' content!

Duration

Owing to the necessity to set up certain cornerstones of the Musketeers plot, this is not a particularly short play. The original production, which included twelve musical numbers, was of two and a half hours duration, including a fifteen minute interval. This is probably quite long enough, especially where audiences predominantly composed of children are concerned. The inclusion of fewer songs is the simplest way to restrict the duration. Seven or eight musical numbers would probably prove quite sufficient for most productions.

There is also quite a high number of individual scenes in this pantomime. Again, this is mainly driven by an approximation of the sequence in which locations occur in *The Three Musketeers* proper. Any production will be greatly assisted by the availability of a forestage playing area, so that shorter scenes can be played out in front of the main tabs, whilst other scenes are changed behind. Lengthy scene changes which interfere with the flow of performance should be avoided if at all possible.

Pace is of paramount importance. Few characters ever have to deliver more than two or three lines at a time—indeed, the overwhelming majority of dialogue is composed of one-liners. These will repay a quick-fire style of playing, and a degree of restraint on the part of those in character roles, who should resist the urge to overly ham up their parts. The snappier the delivery, the harder the material will work for you.

Musical Numbers

The selection of songs is best determined by the society staging the play, influenced as this choice is, by factors such as the type of band/orchestra available, and the singing and dancing talents of the group concerned.

The suggested audience participation song is a mild variant of an old rugby song spoof of *Le Marseillaise*. It is modestly lavatorial in tone. Then again, speaking as a parent of small boys, I can avouch that playground humour from Year One upwards, is almost exclusively lavatorial in tone! If a producing society should deem the proffered song inappropriate, they should of course feel free to adopt material of their own.

The Pantomime Snail

Well, I think it fair to say that you are not likely to come across one of these in your average theatrical hire shop, so you are almost certainly going to have to make your own. This is challenging—but not *too* difficult, and it does provide a wonderful project for an ingenious designer... Should keep them busy for weeks!

In the original production, the pantomime snail was created around a lightweight, timber frame, mounted on small castors. Around this base, a superstructure was constructed from strip metal and chicken wire, fastened together with electrical cable ties, and formed into a reasonable approximation of a snail's body shape. The whole was then covered in lurid green fur fabric—effectively a giant bag. The underside of the tail (both chicken wire and its fur fabric "skin") was left open, so that when the snail was tipped forward, the operator could crawl inside.

The shell, again constructed from battening, strip metal, and chicken wire, was covered with an old sheet soaked in a latex solution, and formed into an appropriate swirl pattern. Once dry, the shell was painted and lacquered, then mounted atop the body section.

The snail was operated by a person kneeling inside the superstructure, who steered and moved the creature by shuffling around on her knees (knee pads essential!) whilst peering through a tiny gauze panel in the snail's "chest". The castors enable the snail to move in any direction, and appear to positively glide! The operator used her hands to operate stalks controlling the eyes.

The eyes are arguably the most essential component, as these endow the creature with its personality. On our creation, the eyes were two suitably painted rubber balls, mounted on a pair of dowel stalks, poking out from the top of the snail's head. By swivelling these around from down below (either simultaneously or independently!), as well as by extending or retracting them, the operator was able to imbue the snail with a quite astonishing degree of expressiveness—to tremendous comic effect.

French Sticks

There is something irresistibly ridiculous about a full-scale mêlée fought with French sticks, especially when accompanied by a wildly inappropriate passage of vainglorious swashbuckling music! Unfortunately, real French sticks will not serve, as they tend to shatter into a thousand breadcrumbs on first impact! For the original production, we manufactured imitation French sticks as follows: Take a 75cm length of 100mm foam rubber pipe cladding. Glue a length of 25mm diameter plastic conduit down the channel in the centre, to provide some additional rigidity. Carve both ends of the resultant baton into rounded tips, and carve out the semblance of a split, crusty top along one surface. Apply several layers of latex solution to the whole piece, then paint appropriate shades of brown. Apply a final coat of clear latex solution to seal.

From more than about ten feet away, the result is pretty convincing and fairly durable. What's more, the protagonists can bash each other with impunity, as the rubber batons really do not hurt! Our sticks lasted several rehearsals and eight performances, requiring only one or two running repairs of extra paint and latex solution. Better still, no laborious fight arranging required—simply go for it!

The Spider

The giant spider which inhabits the pantomime dungeons of The Bastille, requires two identical puppets to be made. Again, this is a delightful project for a handicraft buff. The puppets should be quite large (sort of football sized), and coloured fur fabric is the recommended material. The spiders should have comically scary faces – but should not be genuinely terrifying! Do not underestimate the extent to which arachnophobes can overreact to such things!

The first spider is flown in on a length of fishing line, from directly above the slab on which the unfortunate Constant is confined. This is simply achieved by a member of the stage crew lowering the spider from a preset position overhead, ideally via a small pulley affixed to a beam or some other point above the stage. When this spider's thread is "cut" by Roquefort, the stagehand simply releases the end of the fishing line, and the spider plummets out of sight behind the slab.

The second spider, operated by a puppeteer concealed out of sight behind the slab, now comes into play. If this duplicate spider can be more of a hand puppet (if it can wave its legs at the audience, for instance!) so much the better! The puppeteer needs to withdraw his or her hand, a moment before Zach scoops up the puppet on his shovel, and tosses it away.

One word of warning, avoid the temptation to use black fur fabric to make your spiders—if your dungeon is dimly lit, and unless you are able to deploy a follow spot, they simply won't show up!

The top surface of the slabs themselves should be angled down at 45 degrees towards the floor, rather than horizontal. It is almost impossible to project lines when lying flat on one's back! In the original production, the slabs were manufactured from timber frames, clad in stone-effect wallboard. Black plastic chains attached to slip-on manacles (cut from a length of guttering downpipe) completed the effect.

The True Quiche of Lorraine

You will need to make or acquire a pair of identical boxes to hold the two portions of the fabled True Quiche of Lorraine.

We scratch-built ours from MDF, suitably painted with wood grain effect paint, and adorned with fleur-de-lys decorative mouldings (available from any big DIY store). The cunning part was to install a small green light, powered by a battery, inside each box. The interior of the lid was covered with reflective vinyl, and when each box was opened, a switch activated the light, thus casting an ethereal green glow on the face of the person holding the box! Accompanied by suitably mystical music, this created a neat other-worldly effect.

It has to be said that the batteries and lamp don't leave a lot of room for the quiche—but a small piece of food will suffice, as the audience never really get to see the article in question—except for the point at which the Dame stuffs something from one of the boxes into her mouth... Tests demonstrate that a piece of digestive biscuit provides the optimum effect, in terms of spraying crumbs!

French Characterisation

It is recommended that French accents are avoided, except perhaps where the occasional French phrase or place name occurs.

Not a few jokes contained in this script are made at the expense of our near and dear neighbours, the French. There is absolutely no malice in this material, although in our politically correct times, it is possible that some people may be sensitive to such things. In truth, the prickly relationship across the Channel is part of an ingrained and mutual culture of (largely good-natured) rivalry. This is a populist tradition, which predates pantomime by a *very* long way. I can only say that several French people who came to see the original production avowed that they found it very funny, and took no offence whatsoever. One remarked that the French equally regard the English as a soft target—almost too easy as the butt of many a Gallic joke… Defence rests, M'Lud.

Richard Lloyd

Other pantomimes by Richard Lloyd
published by Samuel French Ltd:

Arabian Knights - the Panto!
The Christmas Cavalier
Smut's Saga or Santa and the Vikings
Treasure Island - the Panto

To C.J.C.A.

ACT I

Scene 1

Paris. The Palais de Justice. The audience chamber of Cardinal Richeleeugh

A claustrophobic space entirely, uniformly red. Red walls, red throne, red dais, red steps. A shaft of light lances through a single, cruciform, slit window high in the wall above the throne, c. A red-robed figure, the Cardinal, sits upon the throne

His henchman, the Chevalier Du Lobster Roquefort enters

Richeleeugh Well? What news?
Roquefort He arrived at first light, your eminence. The prime minister of England made landfall at Calais, as you anticipated.
Richeleeugh In an official capacity?
Roquefort Evidently.
Richeleeugh A likely story. We know the true purpose of this popinjay's visit, do we not, Roquefort?
Roquefort We do, eminence, we do. He will be here in Paris within the hour. I have taken the precaution of standing to the Cardinal's Guard, in readiness.
Richeleeugh Thank you, Roquefort. You may go.
Roquefort Your eminence... (*He bows and turns to go*)
Richeleeugh Oh, Roquefort...
Roquefort (*turning back*) Your eminence?
Richeleeugh Have my other guests arrived?
Roquefort They await your pleasure, eminence.
Richeleeugh Very good. You may admit them.
Roquefort Yes, your eminence.

Roquefort bows again and withdraws

A moment later, two red-robed and hooded figures (Strappado and Bastinado) are admitted to the audience chamber

Richeleeugh God's blessing upon you, brothers. I am Richeleeugh—

Cardinal of France. I heard you were in Paris. The agents of the Holy Inquisition are always welcome in my jurisdiction. Brother Bastinado?

One of the sinister figures inclines its hooded head

And Brother Strappado?

The other figure inclines its head

A pleasure. I am sure I shall have use for your ... singular talents, very soon. (*He throws back his head to roar with evil laughter*) Ha ha ha ha ha ha!!

Lights down

CURTAIN

SCENE 2

Lights up on the forestage

A trapdoor in the stage creaks open, and a dishevelled figure clambers out. It is Plonquer, the thief

Plonquer Poooey! Fresh air at last! Well, Parisian air at any rate. Phew, what a relief! It's no fun living in the sewers, you know! (*He catches sight of the audience*) Ooh, hallo, you lot. Plonquer's the name, thieving's the game. I'm a Parisian vagabond, me. Regular lowlife... That's why I live down there, in the sump, beneath the stews. Now, as it happens, I've got a part in this pantomime—but not for a while yet, so I thought I'd just pop up and say "bonjour"... And if you need me later, just call out "Oi, Plonquer!" and I'll be there in a jiffy. Shall we have a practice? Come on then. After three. One, two, three.

Audience participation

Oh, very good! I can see you're going to enter into the spirit of things! Now, we've got a lot of story to fit into this pantomime, so we don't have time for all that laborious, establishing characters stuff, see. So, why don't I give you a quick run-down on the main players, just so that you know who's who. Then we can cut straight to the chase, right? OK, here we go, then... First of all, the baddies—now, you've already met his malevolence the Cardinal, but let's take another look at his right hand man, Le Chevalier Du Lobster Roquefort.

Act I, Scene 2

Roquefort enters, snarling in his usual fashion

Roquefort Pus-sac! Pus-sac, you moronic oaf!

Throughout the following, Plonquer acts as commentator, addressing the audience directly, and apparently unseen by the other characters

Plonquer Lovely, isn't he? A real nasty piece of work, Le Chevalier.
Roquefort Pus-sac, I say! Get your boil-ridden bottom down here!

Pus-sac scuttles on

Pus-sac Your Grace?
Plonquer Captain Pus-sac, Commandante of the feared Cardinal's Guard.
Roquefort Is everything ready?
Pus-sac (*winking*) Ready as ever, Your Grace.
Roquefort That's what I was afraid of. Everything tickety-boo in the cellars beneath the Palais de Justice? Braziers nice and hot?
Pus-sac You could roast chestnuts on them.
Roquefort I'll be roasting your chestnuts on them if we don't get a result this time! Now get out of my sight, you cretin! Ha ha ha ha!

Audience participation as Pus-sac scurries off

Plonquer (*to the audience*) That's right. You can boo them, 'cos they're nasty rotten villains. And they're not the only ones... Cop a load of this!

Malady De Splinter glides on stage

She and Roquefort recoil slightly as they catch sight of one another

Malady Roquefort!
Roquefort Malady De Splinter... What ill-wind blows you into this gutter?
Malady The same foul, fretting breeze that carried your native charm away on the west wind.
Plonquer As you can see, they don't like each other much.
Roquefort Touché, Mademoiselle Venom.
Malady Now... You have a message for me? From the Cardinal?
Roquefort Not today, thank you. His eminence has new playmates to keep him entertained.
Malady So it's true, then? The Inquisition have made roost in the Palais De Justice.
Roquefort It's true.

Malady What are they doing here?
Roquefort Nobody knows. Not even his eminence—apparently. Better watch your step, Malady. You dance a very fine line, my dear. It would be such a pity to see you slip, and stumble into the tender clutches of the Inquisition.
Malady You'd like that, wouldn't you, Roquefort?
Roquefort Oh no, Malady. I'd love it. Ha ha ha ha!

Audience participation as Roquefort and Malady circle each other like cats, before slinking off in opposite directions

Plonquer Well, that's enough of them. Brrr! Make your skin crawl, don't they? But—what have we here?

Athos, Porthos and Aramis enter to take seats at a tavern table

Aha! At last! The heroes of our little tale. The Three Musketeers themselves! Our garçons principal... Observé, Madames et Monsieurs...

A serving Wench enters, notepad at the ready

Wench Monsieurs...
Athos You! Wench! Brandy!
Wench (*unfazed*) Bonjour, Monsieur Athos.
Athos (*banging the table*) A flask of Cognac, you jade!
Plonquer Le Musketeer Dypsomanique!
Athos Hic!
Wench And for Monsieur Porthos?
Porthos (*roaring*) A haunch of roast venison! (*As an afterthought*) In a fennel and wild artichoke jus, and perhaps with just the suggestion of a tamarind and balsamic vinegar marmalade.
Plonquer Le Musketeer Gastronomique!
Wench And for Monsieur Aramis?
Aramis (*starting*) Mon Dieu! But you're lovely!
Wench (*succinctly, writing on her pad*) "Crêpes".
Aramis (*undeterred*) Surely, by all the Seine, there is no fairer flower than thee.
Wench (*writing*) "Grandes Crêpes".
Aramis Don't be like that... What time d'you knock off, cherie?
Wench Midday.
Aramis See you then?
Wench You're on.

The Wench turns and goes off

Act I, Scene 2   5

Plonquer Le Musketeer Romantique!

Monsieur de Trivialle enters

And of course, their gallant captain, Commandant of the King's Musketeers, Monsieur de Trivialle.
De Trivialle (*bellowing*) You three reprobates!

The Musketeers jump up

Musketeers Oui, mon Capitan!
De Trivialle What are you doing here boozing? The King is on his way! I suppose you've been crawling round the bars of Montmarte all afternoon!
Musketeers Oui, mon Capitan!
De Trivialle Getting blotto on all the cheap wine you can pour down your gaping throats!
Musketeers Oui, mon Capitan!
De Trivialle So now, your greedy bellies are swollen with plonk, and you are fit to burst, huh?
Musketeers Oui, mon Capitan!

The Musketeers exchange glances and make to leave

De Trivialle Hey! Now where are you off to?!
Musketeers Wee wee, mon Capitan!

The Three Musketeers salute hastily, turn and rush off

De Trivialle Hey! Stop! I order you to wait! Duty calls!

Athos enters

Athos (*finishing his drink*) Pardon, mon Capitan… Nature calls! Urrrp!

Athos belches loudly and staggers out after the other two

De Trivialle (*in desperation*) But the King!
Plonquer Ah yes! The King. His most Catholic Majesty, Louis, by the grace of God, King of France!

Louis XIVVVIIXXLIX enters, followed by his Queen, Anne, accompanied by The Duke of Tottenham, and Queen Anne's waiting lady, Constant Hohhi-hon and Malady De Splinter

Louis Ah! Monsieur de Twivialle.
De Trivialle (*bowing*) Your Majesty.
Louis See, De Twivialle, how fortune twavels upon our woyal shoulder ... we have wecently encountered our most beautiful subject, Malady De Splinter.
De Trivialle (*eyeing Malady dubiously*) So I see, Your Majesty. (*He bows*) Malady...
Malady (*inclining her head*) Commandante De Trivialle...

The two eye each other with mutual dislike

Louis But come, De Twivialle—where is the honour guard of our most loyal musketeers?
De Trivialle Um... Caught short, Your Majesty... A, er ... pressing matter...
Louis Of national security?
De Trivialle (*mumbling*) Of the bladder.
Louis Oh... (*Peeved*) We are somewhat disappointed.
De Trivialle (*bowing again*) Your pardon, Majesty.
Louis I twust the wascals are not a-bwawling with those villainous wuffians of the Cardinal's Guard.
De Trivialle Certainly not, Majesty!
Louis Oh. Makes a change. (*He turns to the Queen*) Alas, my love, we have no musketeers to gwace your passage. Nor that of his excellency, the Pwime Minister of Angleterre.
Anne (*pouting prettily*) Oh Louis! Quel fromage! Still, never mind. I'm sure his grace doesn't stand upon ceremony...
Plonquer Her Majesty, Queen Anne.
Anne ...Do you, Totty?
Tottenham What? Eh? Oh! No, no! Not a bit of it!
Plonquer And his grace, The Duke of Tottenham—Prime Minister of England.
Malady Ah, Your Majesty, surely by his handsome presence, the Duke of Tottenham already graces the Queen's passage.
Tottenham (*puffing up*) Oh, I say!
Louis Oh, bwavo, Malady! Bwavo, and then some! Twés gallant!
Plonquer And the wicked Malady is not far wrong either. For they do say, that the moment His Majesty's back is turned——
Anne Oh! Louis! (*She points*) Look over there! An aqueduct!
Louis Good lord! Where?!

As Louis, De Trivialle, and Malady turn away, Queen Anne and Tottenham dive into a passionate, pawing, desperate clinch, with lots of wet, sucking noises

Act I, Scene 2

Plonquer —that the Queen and Tottenham are at it like rabbits on viagra.
Louis (*peering myopically*) We see no aqueduct. Do you, De Twivialle?
De Trivialle I fear not, Majesty.
Louis Malady De Splinter?
Malady Nor I, Your Majesty.
Louis (*bothered*) Stwange, because we can definitely hear slurping, squelching noises.
De Trivialle (*puzzled*) And I, Majesty.
Louis Ah, well... (*He takes De Trivialle by one arm*) You know, De Twivialle, we are fwactionally unsettled by this court tittle-tattle concerning an alleged womance betwixt my dove, the Queen, and his gwace, the Duke of Totten-ham. What say you, Monsieur?
De Trivialle Preposterous, Majesty. They're just chums.
Louis (*to Malady*) Chums?
Malady Well, of course they are. Chums... (*Eyes gleaming*) I mean, look at them now.
Louis What?
Malady (*grating it out at him*) LOOK AT THEM NOW.

Louis turns just in time to see Tottenham and Anne surfacing from their clinch

Louis (*squealing with outrage*) What are you doing?! Unhand her, sir!

The Queen and Tottenham spring apart, looking hopelessly guilty. Constant Hoh-hi-hon smoothly intervenes

Constant Her Majesty had a speck of dust in her perfect blue eyes, Your Majesty. The Duke of Tottenham was just helping to remove it—is that not so, Your Grace?
Plonquer Constant Hoh-hi-hon, wardrobe mistress to the Queen—to the rescue again. Not for the first time. Nor the last, as you shall see.
Tottenham (*blustering*) Abso-ruddy-lutely. Quite correct. Speck of dust. Spot on. Gone now.
Louis Oh. I see. Well. That's alwight then.
Malady (*sotto voce*) Imbecile!
Louis (*aside to Malady*) I agwee. Wuddy Englishman.
Anne (*aside*) Thank you, Constant.
Constant (*aside*) You must be more careful, Majesty, or your secret will be uncovered.
Anne Oh, but Constant, how can I resist him?
Constant You must be strong, Majesty.
Anne But I cannot. I am a weak vessel.
Constant Then I shall be strong for you.

Anne Bless you, Constant.
Malady Ah. Madame Hoh-hi-hon. (*Sotto voce*) Little Miss Perfect... (*Aloud*) Tell me, how does your husband, Monsieur Hoh-hi-hon? (*Acidly*) The snail grower.
Anne (*wide-eyed*) Not just any snail grower, Malady. Snail grower by appointment to the royal court of Versailles.
Malady But of course, Your Majesty.
Constant I regret my poor husband is not entirely well. He spends too much time conversing with his snails. I fear for his state of mind.
Louis Monsieur Hoh-hi-hon has dedicated himself to a quest to gwow the largest edible snail in the histowy of all Fwance! To gwace our woyal table upon the occasion of our wedding anniversary! Is that not so, my petal?
Anne Just so, my fluffy soufflé.
Louis Do you care for snails, Totten-ham?
Tottenham Care for 'em? Good lord, no! Quite attached to me gun dogs, though.
Louis Non, non, non. You mistake, Monsieur. We mean—to eat.
Tottenham (*aghast*) Eat snails?! Good Heavens, no! Can't abide the little blighters. Foreign food don't sit comfortable with the English constitution, doncha know?
Malady No, Your Majesty, (*archly*) but I'll wager His Grace indulges in the occasional nibble on a delectable pair of frog's legs ... is that not so, Your Grace?
Tottenham (*unblinking*) From time to time, Malady. But only in a bed—(*he smiles his devastating smile*) of lettuce.
Malady (*purring*) Naturellment.

The King looks from one to the other in total bafflement, then claps his hands

Louis Come, come... Allez! Allez! We cannot loiter in the stweets all the day long. We have an audience with the Cardinal, do we not, De Twivialle?
De Trivialle Indeed so, Your Majesty. At thwee... (*Catching himself*) Er. I mean three.
Louis Quite so. Quite so. Come along then. En avant! Onward and upward!

All except Plonquer leave

Plonquer And, that's about it. You'll catch up with Monsieur Hoh-hi-hon, the potty purveyor of monster molluscs, very shortly. But now—on with the plot! (*He goes back to his manhole, and starts to climb back down into his sewer*) Oh! First, however... There's just one more person you need to meet. And for that, we must let our gaze wander out from the narrow cobbled streets of Paris and into the remotest corner of faraway Gascony.

Act I, Scene 3

To a mud-caked farmyard, drowning in a stinking sea of pig slurry. Here, you will find the hero of our tale, one D'Artagnan, son of D'Artagnan. And a frustrated Musketeer.

The Lights crossfade to:

SCENE 3

A farmyard in sun-baked Gascony

D'Artagnan, our hero, is shovelling pig manure

D'Artagnan (*singing*) Who wants to be a musketeer?
        I do!
        Wear thigh-length boots and leather gear?
        I do!
        Who wants to——

His aunt, Dame Desirée, enters

Dame NO!
D'Artagnan (*innocently*) What?
Dame No, you are not going off to Paris. No, you are not becoming a musketeer. And no, you are not leaving me here to run this stinkin' pig farm all by meself!
D'Artagnan But auntie Desirée…
Dame "But auntie Desirée" nothing. You're not going. That's final.
D'Artagnan But…
Dame No buts.
D'Artagnan Oh, well, fine.
Dame Good.
D'Artagnan Fine…
Dame Good…

Pause

D'Artagnan (*singing*) Thank heavens, for musketeers—
        They swordfight in the most delightful ways
        Thank heavens, for musketeers—
        They——
Dame NO!
D'Artagnan Auntie, I…

Dame No. No. No. No. And no. Clear enough for you?
D'Artagnan No.
Dame You're not going.
D'Artagnan But I'm a D'Artagnan. Son of D'Artagnan. Grandson of D'Artagnan. Great gr——
Dame Yes, yes. I know the family history. I was there for most of it—worse luck.
D'Artagnan Then you must know that every D'Artagnan lives to be a King's Musketeer.
Dame Yes. And dies shortly afterwards.
D'Artagnan That's beside the point. I have my father's sword.
Dame Yes, dear, you have his nose too, but that won't be any help to you either in a brush with the Cardinal's Guard. Face it, kiddo—you're a reckless puppy. A galloping liability. You wouldn't last a week.
D'Artagnan (*earnestly*) Then help me learn to curb my wild impulses.
Dame I am. Ten years mucking out three hundred prize porkers should put a bit of a damper on the teenage high spirits.
D'Artagnan You know what I mean.
Dame I do. And you're still not going. Now here's a mop and bucket. Slop out those squealing piglets.
D'Artagnan (*peering down to the front row of the audience*) The cubs [or Brownies, or whatever]? But they've only just got here. They're still quite clean.
Dame Don't argue, you tyke. Just get on with it. I'm going to prepare supper.
D'Artagnan Braised pork trotters?
Dame How did you guess?
D'Artagnan It's braised pork trotters every night.
Dame (*shrugging*) That's pig farming.
D'Artagnan Huh! Pig farming! Pork trotters! I'm sick of pigs. In fact—I'm pig sick. Well, I'll show her. I shall go to Paris. I shall become a musketeer. Why, I have my father's sword, the name of his old comrade-in-arms, Monsieur De Trivialle, and an immense bag of pork scratchings. There are no limits to my horizons! So here goes! (*He slaps his thigh*)

Song 1

After the song, D'Artagnan exits

A few seconds later, the Dame enters

Dame D'Artagnan! Where has that boy got to now? You didn't see him go, did you?

Audience participation

Did you? Where'd he slope off to then? Paris?! To become a musketeer? Why the disobedient little scallywag! Honestly, ladies and gentlemen, boys and girls, the cheek I have to put up with! I'm sure most little boys aren't this naughty, are they?

Audience participation

Are they? Well, as a D'Artagnan, I am left with no option. I shall have to go after him! (*She calls over her shoulder*) Pigs—look to thyselves! Gay Paree—here I come!

Jaunty French music. Lights down

Scene 4

A tavern outside Paris

D'Artagnan enters and sits at a table

D'Artagnan The last inn before Paris. I shall rest awhile before entering the city, and tarry over an honest repast of bread and cheese, washed down by good country wine. My, but this is a peaceful spot...

Drum

There is the sudden menacing tramp of military footwear, and a company of the Cardinal's Guard march in, led by Le Chevalier Du Lobster Roquefort

He calls them to a halt outside the tavern. The Guards break into a snappy and completely inappropriate little dance routine before being dismissed by Roquefort

Roquefort Cardinal's Guard ... fall—OUT!

The Guards all immediately start squabbling with each other

No, you boneheads! I mean—dismiss.

The Guards immediately start dismissing what he has said, with comments like: "oh, he's always saying that..." and "oh, he doesn't mean it really"

(*Exasperated*) Look! Just get lost, will you!

The Guards all shrug Gallically, and start to wander off

Roquefort catches the last two and pulls them back—it is Zoot A Lor and Zach Rebleur

> Not you two! I fancy there is some garbage to be disposed of. (*He kicks the table at which D'Artagnan is sitting*) Hey you! Shift your scrawny bottom, you oik!
> **D'Artagnan** Excuse me?
> **Roquefort** This is my table.
> **D'Artagnan** I think not.
> **Roquefort** Look. I have a private meeting—with a lady.
> **D'Artagnan** She has my sympathy.
> **Roquefort** You provincial dung beetle!
> **D'Artagnan** What did you call me?
> **Roquefort** A dung beetle. Want to make something of it?
> **D'Artagnan** Not that. You said I was from Provence!
> **Roquefort** (*patiently*) No, I said you were provincial.
> **D'Artagnan** Just as I thought. (*He slaps Roquefort with his glove*) I am a Gascon.
> **Roquefort** (*to the audience*) It gets worse…
> **D'Artagnan** And soon to be a King's Musketeer.
> **Roquefort** Worse and worse…
> **D'Artagnan** I shall fillet you with the sword of my father.
> **Roquefort** (*sneering*) Well, pardon me for not quaking.
> **D'Artagnan** Draw.
> **Roquefort** I really don't have time for this.
> **D'Artagnan** Draw your sword, Monsieur!
> **Roquefort** I am the finest swordsman in all France.
> **D'Artagnan** And the biggest jackanapes in this tavern.
> **Roquefort** Er … no, I think that's you actually.
> **D'Artagnan** What?
> **Roquefort** Take a look behind you.
> **D'Artagnan** Where? (*He turns*)

Roquefort thwacks him across the head with a cosh he slips from his sleeve

> **Roquefort** See?

D'Artagnan collapses on to the table. Roquefort gestures to Zoot and Zach

> All right. Take this Gascon pig's dropping and throw him down the well. That should cool his temper. Hup! I'll take that. (*He relieves D'Artagnan*

Act I, Scene 4   13

of his sword, snaps it in two, and replaces the hilt portion in its scabbard) There! Your filleting days are over, my young friend—before they have even begun. (*He gestures to Zach and Zoot to carry out the unconscious D'Artagnan*)

As Zach and Zoot go off, Malady De Splinter glides on

Ah—the lovely Malady.
Malady Eurrgh—the repellent Roquefort.
Roquefort (*hissing*) One day, Malady, I shall have you at a disadvantage.
Malady In your dreams, bucko.
Roquefort You have information for his eminence?
Malady Might have…
Roquefort Proceed.
Malady The Queen and The Duke of Tottenham are at it.
Roquefort At what?
Malady It.
Roquefort Morbleu! You are certain?
Malady I saw it with my own eyes.
Roquefort I must notify his eminence.
Malady Do so. Adieu.

Malady and Roquefort exit in different directions

A second later, the Dame enters

Dame Well, here we are … the last tavern before Paris, and not a sign of D'Artagnan. Honestly, that boy is such an enfant terrible!

Zach and Zoot enter, dusting their hands

Zach Well done, Zoot—straight down the chute.
Zoot And no way back—nice one, Zach!
Dame Excusé moi, mes bràves—but I don't suppose you happen to have seen my nephew D'Artagnan, have you?
Zoot Not a short lad? Brown hair?
Dame Yes!
Zach Brown eyes?
Dame Yes!
Zoot Brown doublet?
Dame That's it!
Zach Brown feather in his hat?
Dame Yes! Yes!

Zach Haven't seen him.
Dame Oh.
Zoot (*tugging at Zach's sleeve*) Yes, we have. We dropped him down the well just now.
Dame Eh?!
Zach No. No. That wasn't him. Look—does your nephew have a great lump on his bonce, the size of a goose's egg?
Dame No. No, he doesn't.
Zach There you are, then. Told you it wasn't him.
Dame Oh. Right, then. Well, thanks anyway.
Zach Not a problem. C'mon, Zoot.

Zach and Zoot start to go off—but the Dame has spied something on the ground

Dame Wait a minute—what's this?
Zoot (*peering over her shoulder*) That's a button.
Dame It's his button!
Zach Is it? How do you know?
Dame Because it bears our family crest—look!
Zach That's a pig.
Dame Yes. Rampant.
Zoot I knew a woman like that once.
Zach Rampant?
Zoot No—face like a pig.
Dame So he was here!
Zach Well, he'll be in Paris by now. We're only ten minutes from the city gates here.
Dame You're right! I'd better get after him.
Zach I should if I were you.
Dame I've got to find him before he does something reckless and lands himself in trouble.
Zach Oh dear! That would never do.
Dame Certainly wouldn't. Well, cheerio then.

The Dame goes off

Zach Ta ta!

Zach and Zoot look at each other, shrug, and wander off singing

Zach & Zoot(*singing*) "Ding Dong Bell!
        The Gascon's down a well…

Act I, Scene 5   15

>   If someone doesn't pull him out
>   He's going to start to smell...

Lights down

Scene 5

The Palais De Justice. The audience chamber of Cardinal Richeleeugh

The Cardinal and Roquefort enter

Richeleeugh So, it is true then. The Queen and The Duke of Tottenham are entangled in a *liaison dangereuse.*

Roquefort So it appears, eminence.

Richeleeugh Just as I suspected. But how to prove it, Roquefort? That is the question.

Roquefort To what end, your eminence?

Richeleeugh The King needs to be taught a lesson, Roquefort. He allows that babbling airhead the Queen to sway what little judgement he has in affairs of state. His Majesty needs a sharp reminder, Roquefort, that I, Richeleeugh, am the true power behind the throne of France.

Roquefort But how, your eminence? The Queen covers her tracks like a practiced deceiver.

Richeleeugh No, Roquefort. The Queen is too stupid. It is her interfering wardrobe mistress, the delectable Madame Hoh-hi-hon, who orchestrates this affair—you may be sure of it.

Roquefort Shall I bring her in for interrogation?

Richeleeugh Don't be stupid, Roquefort. The Queen would smell a rat.

Roquefort I could wear deodorant.

Richeleeugh I mean, imbecile, that Her Majesty would suspect. No... We must find a more subtle line of attack. Someone close to the wardrobe mistress, perhaps.

Roquefort Monsieur Hoh-hi-hon?

Richeleeugh The snail grower?

Roquefort We could lean on him.

Richeleeugh He'd snap like a rotten twig. (*After a pause*) Good idea, Roquefort. Draw up the warrant.

Roquefort And if we succeed in this affair, your eminence—what will become of the Queen?

Richeleeugh For her betrayal of the King? Why, that would constitute High Treason, Roquefort—would it not?

Roquefort Most assuredly, eminence.

Richeleeugh Impeachment then—and the headsman's axe.
Roquefort And the Duke of Tottenham?
Richeleeugh (*distantly*) The same.
Roquefort But that would mean war, eminence!
Richeleeugh (*eyes suddenly blazing*) Precisely! War with England! The very sport I seek!
Roquefort And the prize, eminence?
Richeleeugh Conquest, Roquefort. The complete subjugation of England by the armies of France!
Roquefort Why, your eminence?
Richeleeugh Why? Because I hate the English, and everything about them, that's why! Their stiff upper lips and their mammoth boot fairs, their mother of parliaments and their chicken tikka pizzas. I detest them. Oh no... When I rule England, Roquefort, there's going to be a few changes, you mark my words. Forget roast beef—it's going to be horsemeat for lunch, tea and dinner! And no more crisp, juicy red apples from the garden of England either—only nice, pappy, French apples with the consistency and flavour of wet toilet paper.

Audience participation

   The children of England shall be compelled to dress in clothes which are at least twenty years out of date—like French teenagers!

Audience participation

   That's right. And wear silly little knapsacks on their backs!

Audience participation

   Sharp, yellow, flavoursome, English mustard will be replaced with the mildly unpleasant brown slop that is French mustard!

Audience participation

   And what is more, we shall abolish the famous English sense of fair play. We shall force them to play football like the French—to take a dive the moment they set foot in the penalty area; to complain bitterly when they lose—and to gloat spitefully when they win!

Audience participation

   And—the pièce de résistance! The ultimate indignity! Every genteel,

Act I, Scene 6   17

flushing English lavatory shall be ripped out and replaced with two bricks and a putrid hole in the floor!

Audience participation

Oh, you can squeal all you like, you pitiful English milksops! But you'll thank me one day, when I've made proper Frenchmen of the lot of you! After all, you'd far rather be French than English really—wouldn't you!

Audience participation

Oh, yes, you would...

Audience participation

Well, too bad. Because if I get my way—you're going to be! And I always get my way! Ha ha ha ha ha!!

They descend into manic villainous cackling, leading to:

Song 2

Scene 6

Paris. A street without the Headquarters of The King's Musketeers

Monsieur De Trivialle enters, followed by D'Artagnan

De Trivialle Well, young D'Artagnan, you certainly are the spitting image of your father. But I regret it is not possible to enrol you into the Corps Des Musketeers at present.
D'Artagnan But Monsieur De Trivialle, I have come all the way from Gascony. I have my father's sword, and——
De Trivialle Yes, I know—an immense bag of pork scratchings. You told me.
D'Artagnan But my father's sword, Monsieur...
De Trivialle Alas, possession of the name D'Artagnan and an old sword are not in themselves qualifications enough to become a King's Musketeer.
D'Artagnan And the immense bag of pork scratchings?
De Trivialle Carries little weight.
D'Artagnan But Monsieur! I am wilfully headstrong, and reckless to a fault.
De Trivialle That may not count entirely in your favour.
D'Artagnan What must I do?

De Trivialle You must perform a feat of supreme heroism, courage, and gallantry. An act which will make all France cry "Bravo!"
D'Artagnan (*downcast*) I see.
De Trivialle Think you can you do it?
D'Artagnan (*rallying*) Of course. I am a D'Artagnan!

Durning the following, Athos wanders on and ends up swaying unnoticed beside D'Artagnan

De Trivialle (*smiling*) That's the spirit. Well, cut along then. And—hey! Try to control that Gascon temper!

De Trivialle strides off

Athos throws his head back to drain the last drips from an upturned bottle

D'Artagnan Temper, huh! Silly old fool! I'll show him! (*He turns and walks straight into Athos*)
Athos Hey. Watch it.
D'Artagnan Watch it yourself, you raddled old wino.
Athos Easy, Tiger. Want a swig?
D'Artagnan No, thank you.
Athos Suit yourself. (*Half aside*) Snotty little squab.
D'Artagnan What did you call me?
Athos A snotty little squab … a baby pigeon in a stuffed shirt.
D'Artagnan I demand satisfaction.
Athos Can't help you there, sunshine. But there's a passable bordello on the Rue Des Banques.
D'Artagnan I'm talking rapiers at dawn.
Athos Oh, I see. A duel! (*He regards him in bleary puzzlement*) But then I'd have to kill you.
D'Artagnan You can try. Name the place.
Athos Oh, all right. The Tavern Contretemps in St Germain.
D'Artagnan Three o' clock?
Athos Suits me. They're open all day.
D'Artagnan Fine. See you then.

D'Artagnan exits

Athos Okey-doke… (*He shouts after him*) Mine's a large cognac. (*To himself*) Nutter…

Lights down, then up on another part of the stage, where Porthos is sitting down to lunch. An innkeeper has just placed a loaded plate in front of him

Act I, Scene 6

Innkeeper Monsieur Porthos—your goujons aux foie gras, refreshed with a chilled lime and basil vinaigrette. Just as you ordered.
Porthos (*consulting his pocket watch*) Midday. Excellent. I've been looking forward to this since elevenses.
Innkeeper Bon appetit!

As Porthos is tucking his napkin into his shirt front, Le Chevalier Du Lobster Roquefort walks past his table and out through the audience

A moment later, D'Artagnan charges on in hot pursuit

D'Artagnan Hey! Stop that man! He's the villain who clobbered me this morning.
Porthos Young man. I am trying to have a civilised lunch. If you don't stop shouting, I shall clobber you this afternoon.
D'Artagnan (*peering over the audience*) Which way did he go?! Drat! I can't see over all these people! Excusé moi! (*He places one hand on Porthos's shoulder, and leaps on to the table to scan the area*)
Porthos (*amazed*) You trod on my goujons.
D'Artagnan I'm sorry. That must have been painful.
Porthos (*outraged*) And you're standing in my foie gras, you lumbering lummox!
D'Artagnan (*jumping down*) Your pardon, Monsieur. I'm in a hurry.
Porthos Hup! (*He catches his arm*) Not good enough. I demand satisfaction.
D'Artagnan Well, there's a bonking shop in the Rue Des Bordellos. I'm told it's very good.
Porthos Satisfaction involving rapiers, you blundering haybale.
D'Artagnan Very well. Name the place.
Porthos The Tavern Contretemps in St Germain—three o'clock.
D'Artagnan Erm... Couldn't make it quarter past, could you?
Porthos Fine. I'll have time for a light snack beforehand.
D'Artagnan See you there.
Porthos Better had... (*He regards the ruin of his foie gras*) Philistine.

D'Artagnan dashes off

Lights down. Scene changes to another part of the stage. Lights up

Aramis stands in a rose-wreathed archway, the tavern wench he was chatting up earlier is in his arms

Aramis Ah, cherie, I have waited for this moment for ever.
Wench But Monsieur Aramis, I've only known you since this morning.
Aramis Ah! What are days and weeks where true love is concerned?

Wench True love?! (*Swooning*) Oh, Monsieur Aramis...
Aramis The moment where our lips touch, our sweat mingles—and our hearts collide.
Wench (*swooning some more*) Oh, Monsieur Aramis...
Aramis (*throatily*) Oh, cherie...

D'Artagnan barges on between them, sending the Wench sprawling

D'Artagnan Oh, get out of the way, will you!
Wench Oh!
Aramis What the...?
D'Artagnan (*grabbing Aramis by the collar*) You haven't seen him, have you? Tall, ill-favoured fellow... I swear he came this way.
Wench (*picking herself off the floor*) Men!

The Wench runs off

D'Artagnan Merde! I've lost the villain!
Aramis Merde! I've lost my snog!
D'Artagnan I'll try back the other way.
Aramis You sir!
D'Artagnan Who, me?
Aramis Yes—you! You galumphing galoot! You just came between myself and a lady.
D'Artagnan Don't tell me... Satisfaction?
Aramis You bet.
D'Artagnan Have you tried the Rue des Bonks?
Aramis (*correcting him*) Banques. (*After a pause*) Been there—done that.
D'Artagnan St Germain then. The Tavern Contretemps?
Aramis Three o'clock?
D'Artagnan Er ... no.
Aramis Quarter past?
D'Artagnan Can't.
Aramis Half past then?
D'Artagnan Fine.
Aramis Sorted.
D'Artagnan See you then.

Aramis stalks off

D'Artagnan turns to the audience

Well... I think that all went rather well.

Black-out

Scene 7

A slightly different street in Paris

The Dame enters

Dame Well, here we are—Paris. World Capital of Romance! (*She peers around herself*) What a grothole... And I'm bloomin' well starving! Me stomach thinks me throat's been cut! Oh, ladies, what I wouldn't give for a coq au vin. Or a plate of braised pig's trotters. (*She moves down to the audience*) Ere, I say... D'you like pig's trotters?

Audience participation

Oh, we eat all sorts of things, we French do. Like blackbirds, and frogs, and chocolate-covered earwigs! We do! It's true, I tell you! But best of all—snails! Yes, that's right, boys and girls—snails! All smothered in garlic butter. Delicious!

Audience participation

You English, you don't know what you're missing! Here, I tell you what though—I bet you'd rather eat a snail than have a snail eat you, wouldn't you?! Oh, yes, you would!

Audience participation

Can you imagine that, eh—a snail big enough to eat a person? It'd have to be blinkin' enormous, wouldn't it?! Have you ever seen such a thing?!

An enormous pantomime snail enters behind her, and makes its slow progress across the stage

Audience participation throughout the following

You have?
Have you?
Where?
Behind me?
No, there's nothing behind me—you're just pulling my leg...
You are. You're pulling my leg...
I'll take a look, shall I?
Eeek! A man-eating mollusc! Help!

A disreputable-looking old codger scuttles on—the famed Monsieur Hoh-hi-hon

Hoh-hi-hon (*to the snail*) Gérard! There you are! (*To the Dame*) Thank God you found him!
Dame Gérard?
Hoh-hi-hon My prize snail—Gérard Drippy-Dew.
Dame Drippy-Dew! Why d'you call him Drippy-Dew?
Hoh-hi-hon Madame, have you seen what he leaves behind him?
Dame Eee-yuch! That's slimier than a Cardinal's handshake.
Hoh-hi-hon Please! Take care what you say! The agents of the Cardinal are everywhere. (*Hissing*) The walls have ears.
Dame Do they?

A large pink ear snaps out from the side of a nearby wall

So they do... Who are you, then?
Hoh-hi-hon Hoh-hi-hon.
Dame Yes, dear, very Gallic, but what's your name?
Hoh-hi-hon That is my name. Henri Hubért Hoh-hi-hon, at your service. Purveyor of fine snails to the Royal Court of Versailles.
Dame I see.
Hoh-hi-hon Gérard is the fruit of a lifetime's quest to cultivate the world's largest edible snail.
Dame Edibubble! You're never going to eat Gérard!
Hoh-hi-hon Ssssshhhhh! Madame, please! He is very sensitive, Gérard. You might not guess, but beneath that hard outer shell, he's just a great big softie.
Dame Yes, I can imagine— (*she shudders*) unfortunately.

Gérard starts to slither off

Hey-up! Where's he off to then?
Hoh-hi-hon You've upset him.
Dame Moves quite fast for a snail, doesn't he?!
Hoh-hi-hon Relative to his size—not particularly. Ordinary garden snails can move very fast, you know.
Dame Really? How fast?
Hoh-hi-hon Well, it depends how hard you throw them.
Dame What does he eat?
Hoh-hi-hon Anything he can get his sucker on... the more rotten the better, preferably.
Dame Well, don't let him near the jokes in this show then... They're pretty rotten. Oooh! What's he doing now?

Act I, Scene 7

Hoh-hi-hon Ah! Observé...

Gérard shudders a few times and produces a large wobbly ball of jelly from his rear end

Dame (*recoiling*) Snail poo!
Hoh-hi-hon Non! It's an egg! Morbleu! He's laid an egg!
Dame Wait a sec! How can Gérard have laid an egg? I mean—he's a he, isn't he?
Hoh-hi-hon Non! Non! Snails are hermaphrodite—neither entirely male nor female.
Dame Really? (*To the audience*) I know how he feels.
Hoh-hi-hon Come, quickly, we must get the egg back to my laboratory. I think we should incubate it.
Dame Well, I certainly don't fancy it poached in a glass of milk.

Gérard makes it offstage

Hoh-hi-hon Come... Quickly...
Dame All right! Hang on a minute! I've only just arrived, and I haven't sorted out anywhere to stay yet.
Hoh-hi-hon Well, you can lodge with me!
Dame Er, yes, well, that's very nice of you, but I'm not sure I want to stay in a house full of moist crawly things.
Hoh-hi-hon Oh, don't worry about the wife—she won't mind.
Dame I didn't mean... (*With an astonished double-take*) You've got a wife?
Hoh-hi-hon Huh! Not that you'd know it. She's never there, the minx. Too busy sucking up to the Queen.
Dame Sucking up? Wait a minute. You're not married to a snail, are you?
Hoh-hi-hon Hardly. Constant Hoh-hi-hon is the most desirable sex-kitten in all Paris. (*Confidingly*) Trouble is, she doesn't understand me.
Dame (*darkly*) Can't imagine why...
Hoh-hi-hon Inconceivable, n'est pas?! Come on, I'll tell you all about it on the way.
Dame (*depressed*) Oh, good... (*She shrugs helplessly to the audience*)

The Dame and Hoh-hi-hon trudge off in pursuit of Gérard

Lights down

SCENE 8

The Tavern Contretemps in St Germain—and a seedy dive, if ever there was one

D'Artagnan enters to find the dingy taproom deserted, except for the burly landlord, wiping down his bar

D'Artagnan Well, this is the place. The Tavern Contretemps.
Landlord Hey, you! Leave your sword outside.
D'Artagnan A Gascon is never parted from his sword.
Landlord Listen, mon bràve, when you run a tavern named in honour of an argument, you don't allow edged weapons into the saloon. Either the sword goes, or you do.
D'Artagnan But here come my appointments, and Morbleu! They're all together!

The Three Musketeers enter the taproom, sighting D'Artagnan simultaneously

Athos The snotty little squab!
Porthos The lumbering lummox!
Aramis The galumphing galoot!
Porthos My galumphing galoot, Aramis—I have reserved the pleasure of puncturing this conceited tadpole's self-confidence at a quarter past three.
Athos Porthos, you cannot possibly be fighting him at a quarter past—because I will have killed him by one minute past the hour!
Aramis Wrong, mes amis! It is I who will be giving this streeturchin a lesson in manners—at half past three.
Athos No chance! (*To D'Artagnan*) Tell them, Tinkerbell—I am first, am I not?
D'Artagnan Tinkerbell! (*He angrily sweeps his broken sword from its sheath*) Ready when you are, you drink-sodden barfly.
Landlord Oi! You! Outside!
Aramis Don't worry, Maurice. Our young firebrand appears to have been caught short.
D'Artagnan (*aghast*) My father's sword!
Aramis Well, half of it, anyway.
D'Artagnan Oh no! How did that happen?!
Porthos Well, it appears that had you crossed swords with him, Athos—you'd have ended up half-cut.
Aramis Which would be an agreeable change from totally bladdered.
Athos (*pleasantly*) Up yours, my sworn companions.

Act I, Scene 8

Porthos What are you playing at, young man? It's very bad form to arrange three duels in one afternoon, and then turn up with a broken rapier.
D'Artagnan Lend me a sword. I shall fight you one by one.
Porthos You certainly shall not. We three shall fight you all at once—just on the off chance that you are half as dangerous as you are impetuous!
D'Artagnan But that's not fair!
Porthos (*amazed*) Fair?! Please! Let's remember we're French, after all.
D'Artagnan Oh, yes. Sorry.
Aramis Right, then. Shall we step outside?

There is a sudden kerfuffle at the doorway, and Pus-sac and a party of Guards burst in

Athos The Cardinal's Guard!
Pus-sac Well well! Musketeers... And about to engage in a duel unless I'm much mistaken. Thereby contravening the bye-laws of Paris.
Aramis Hey! It's Pustule, isn't it?
Athos Pus-bag, surely.
Porthos Bag-puss.
Pus-sac Capitan Pus-sac to you, you insolent dogs.
Innkeeper Hey! You! No swords in my bar!
Pus-sac It's all right, landlord—we parked our blades outside. Besides, we won't need swords to take in three pansies like this.
D'Artagnan Four pansies!
Aramis Wait a moment.
D'Artagnan No. I insist. I am D'Artagnan of Gascony. It's my duel too, and I'm damn well going to be busted for it!
Porthos We're none of us going to be busted, you tempestuous pipsqueak! We are going to resist arrest.
D'Artagnan Are we?
Athos Too right.
Aramis All right, Pus-bag. Three of the King's Musketeers—and the Mouth of the Dordogne here—against five of the Cardinal's playground bullies. Fancy your chances, do you?
Pus-sac (*sneering*) Well, I don't fancy yours much. A guttersnipe, a sot, a fop, and a fatboy. What *are* they going to make of you down at the Palais de Justice...?
Athos You'll have to take us first—coppeur.
Pus-sac All right. Want to play hard-boules? Have it your own way!
D'Artagnan But our swords... (*Correcting himself*) Well, your swords. They're outside.
Porthos Fear not, young Gascon, the landlord will provide.

The Landlord stomps between the two groups, carrying a huge covered basket, which he bangs down on to table between them. He whisks off the cloth, before stepping back out of the way

Landlord Gentlemen—choose your weapons!
D'Artagnan (*peering at the basket in amazement*) French sticks?!
Porthos What else? This is Paris, after all. (*Selecting a loaf*) Gentlemen—to arms!
D'Artagnan (*to the audience*) Crumbs!

Each combatant seizes up a loaf, and springs to the en garde position

Pus-sac En garde!
Aramis (*to the audience*) En croute, actually.
Porthos Ah! (*Sternly*) Monsieurs—you forget yourselves. Does not his eminence train his curs to utter Grace before breaking bread?
Pus-sac Prayers won't help you, fatso.
Porthos Indulge me.
Pus-sac (*sneering*) Go ahead.

All snatch off their hats and dutifully bow their heads

Porthos (*piously*) Our Lord, which art in Heaven, give us this day our daily bread... (*He slyly looks up, and winks at Athos and Aramis. Shouting*) And bash the numbnuts with it!!
Musketeers HUZZA!

The Musketeers joyously launch themselves upon the unsuspecting Cardinal's Guards—with D'Artagnan following. A furious mêlée ensues. As the weapons are only French sticks, this requires absolutely no fight-arranging whatsoever—the participants simply bash each other to their hearts' content! By the end of the brawl, however, Pus-sac and his men are forced to withdraw, half-carrying, half-dragging, one of their number

Pus-sac You haven't heard the last of this! You flouncing fondant fancies!
Aramis (*jeering*) The trouble with you, Pus-bag, is that you don't use your loaf!
Athos The fellow's just ill-bred.
Porthos Well, he's certainly not upper crust.
Pus-sac You'll be sorry for this!

Pus-sac's exit is accompanied by the jeers and catcalls of the Musketeers and D'Artagnan

Act I, Scene 8   27

Aramis Well, young D'Artagnan, you acquitted yourself like a true musketeer.
D'Artagnan Alas, Monsieur, I would be a Musketeer in truth, as my father was before me. But first I must undertake a feat of supreme heroism, courage, and gallantry.
Porthos One step at a time, lad. You'll achieve your dream—if you want it badly enough.

Song 3

Athos This calls for a celebration! Landlord! Bring wine!
Porthos What a team! Together, we four are unstoppable!
Athos A legend in the making!
Aramis What we need now is a motto.
Athos Something catchy.
Porthos I know—how about: (*he strikes a pose*) "All For One"!

Pause. The others look at him

Aramis Is that it?
Porthos What's wrong with that?
Aramis It's a bit concise, isn't it? Shouldn't it be: "All For One, And—Something Something Something"?
D'Artagnan It ought to be: "All For One, And One For Something".
Athos D'Artagnan's right. How about: "All For One, And One For The Road"!
Aramis Trust you...
Porthos "All For One, And One Flew Over The Cuckoo's Nest"?
All (*derisively*) No.
Athos "All For One, And One, Two, Three O'clock, Four O'clock, Rock"?
Porthos Not catchy enough.
Aramis "All For One, And Once More Unto The Breach Dear Friends, Once More!"
Porthos Well, yes, that's good. Suitably heroic. But somehow—a little too English.
All (*mumbling their agreement*) Hmmmm...
D'Artagnan Wait! I've got it! "All For One—And One For All!"
All (*thoughtfully, to themselves*) "All For One, And One For All"...

They stand and thrust their French sticks skyward

(*Shouting*) ALL FOR ONE, AND ONE FOR ALL!!

They slap their thighs in ear-splitting unison

Pause

Athos (*darkly*) It'll never catch on.

Black-out

Scene 9

The King's audience chamber

Louis and De Trivialle enter

Louis It won't do, De Twivialle. It simply won't wash! I will not have the Gentlemen of my Woyal Bodyguard, scwapping with the Cardinal's wuffians in second-wate hostelwies!

De Trivialle I believe the Musketeers to have been grievously provoked, Your Majesty.

Louis Thank Heavens no-one was killed. Do we understand one of the Guards suffered a slight concussion?

De Trivialle I'm afraid so, Your Majesty.

Louis A glancing blow fwom a wapier, no doubt?

De Trivialle No, Sire. A baguette.

Louis A baguette!? Are you telling me, De Twivialle, that this scwimmage was decided by the cut and thwust of bweadsticks?!

De Trivialle More or less. A bunfight—in which the Cardinal's men turned out to be half-baked croissants.

Louis No wonder his eminence is spitting cwoutons. Honestly, De Twivialle, I can hardly bear to be in the same Palace with the man at the moment. His eminence wears a face like the clenched bottom of a wombat.

De Trivialle (*drily*) I fear that is the Cardinal's customary expression, Majesty.

Louis Now now, De Twivialle. A little wespect, s'il vous plait! Now, tell me of this young wascal you have taken under your wing.

De Trivialle D'Artagnan, Your Majesty. I served with his father in the Gascon Cadets.

Louis A dependable soldier, De Twivialle? A solid fellow, your old comwade?

De Trivialle No Majesty—a complete lunatic. Mad as the March hare. Morbleu! But I loved him like a brother. What a swordsman! No finer blade in the Kingdom.

Act I, Scene 9

Louis And the son shares the gift, eh? An artist in tempered steel. A virtuoso in the intwicate dwama of mortal combat.
De Trivialle No indeed, Sire. He has all the poise, grace and charm of a baby rhinoceros.
Louis (*dubiously*) I see...
De Trivialle But his heart is purer than the high snows of Mont Blanc. And he lives only to serve you, Majesty.
Louis And so he shall, De Twivialle. So he shall. Loyalty is a ware commodity in a man, and shall be wecompensed.
De Trivialle I have the fellows outside, Your Majesty.
Louis Alwighty. Wheel the wascals in.

Whilst the Musketeers and D'Artagnan are ushered into the King's presence, Louis strikes what he considers to be the heroic pose of a commander-in-chief

Well boys!
All (*bowing low*) Your Majesty...
Louis Don't you "Your Majesty" me, you wagabonds! We are vewy, vewy cwoss wiv you. Observé... (*He jumps up and down and bellows*) WE ARE IN A WEGULAR WANTING WOYAL WAGE! (*He calms down a little and turns to the Musketeers*) There now! Do you know what that was?
Musketeers (*nonplussed*) No, Your Majesty.
Louis Ha! Tell them, De Twiv.
De Trivialle (*embarrassed*) That was the madness of King Louis (*pronouncing the letters*) XXVLIXIII.VXI.
Louis Just so! Quite! So—just you watch it before you go mixing it wiv the Cardinal's wuffnecks again, understand me?
Musketeers (*gravely*) Yes, Your Majesty.
Louis Alwight then. Now. Here are forty silver pistoles to be shared equally amongst you.
Musketeers Thank you, Your Majesty!
Louis Yes, well, make sure the Gascon weceives a decent meal, good lodgings, and smartens himself up a bit! He's going to have to do something about his wardwobe if he's going to be a Musketeer.

D'Artagnan leaps forward, his eyes shining with hope

D'Artagnan A Musketeer, Majesty?!
Louis (*taken aback*) Well—once you have performed a feat of supweme hewoism, couwage, and gallantwy, natuwally.
D'Artagnan (*crestfallen*) Oh—I see. Of course.
Louis Yes. Well. Cut along. No time like the pwesent, you know.

D'Artagnan No, Your Majesty.

D'Artagnan and the Musketeers step forward on to the forestage as the curtains begin to close behind them on the King and De Trivialle

Louis (*calling after him*) We wecommend you engage yourself a valet, young man.

The curtains close. D'Artagnan turns to the Musketeers

D'Artagnan A valet?
Porthos He means a manservant.
Aramis To look after your wardrobe, your grooming, your toilette.
Athos To fetch your cognac.
Porthos And prepare your meals.
Aramis But most of all—to watch your back.
Porthos To show you the ropes.
Athos And to fetch your cognac.
Porthos Someone who knows their way around.
Aramis Who knows all the dodges.
Athos And who knows where they keep the best cognac.
Aramis In short...
Porthos A Parisian vagabond.
Aramis A regular lowlife.
Porthos See you later, mon ami.
Athos Salut!

The Three Musketeers wander off

D'Artagnan A Parisian vagabond! A regular lowlife! But where on earth am I to find such a creature?
Athos (*calling back*) Try the sewers...
D'Artagnan The sewers! (*To the audience*) Excuse me, but—look, I don't suppose you happen to know any vagabonds, do you?

Audience participation

You do?! Who?

Audience participation

Oh... Will you give him a shout for me? After three, then ... un, deux, trois...

Act I, Scene 9

Audience participation

The manhole flips open, and Plonquer pops his head up

Plonquer Somebody call?
D'Artagnan Hallo. You must be Plonquer.
Plonquer Allo. You must be desperate.
D'Artagnan What for?
Plonquer To call me. Don't you know I'm a good-for-nothing vagabond?
D'Artagnan Just what I'm looking for. How'd you like to be my valet?
Plonquer (*starting to retreat down his manhole*) No, thanks.
D'Artagnan No! Wait! I can make it worth your while.
Plonquer (*his greed kindled*) Whatcha got then?
D'Artagnan My father's sword ... broken.
Plonquer Yerrrrrs.
D'Artagnan An immense bag of pork scratchings.
Plonquer Go on.
D'Artagnan And a reckless disregard for danger.
Plonquer (*disappearing back into his manhole*) I'm not interested.

The manhole bangs shut

D'Artagnan (*loudly*) And ten silver pistoles.

Pause

The manhole flips open again. Plonquer pops his head up

Plonquer When do I start?
D'Artagnan Right now. I need to find lodgings. Tonight.
Plonquer (*jumping out of his manhole*) No problem. Monsieur Hoh-hi-hon keeps rooms above his snail farm in the Rue de Bon Voyages.
D'Artagnan All right. What are we waiting for?
Plonquer Well, for you to tell me your name, actually.
D'Artagnan Oh. Sorry. D'Artagnan, I'm a Gascon.
Plonquer Plonquer. I'm only lowlife. (*He extends a grimy hand to D'Artagnan*) But I'm your lowlife.

They shake hands. Lights down

Scene 10

The Louvre Palace. The boudoir of Queen Anne

Anne and Tottenham enter with Constant in attendance

Anne This is lunacy! You should not have come, My Lord.
Tottenham Dash it all, Anne. I had to see you.
Anne But you were supposed to take ship for England this morning. The Cardinal suspects—I am sure of it! If Louis discovers you are still in Paris tonight, it will be *finis* for both of us.
Tottenham But hang it all, Anne, I love you, d'you see?
Anne I beg you, My Lord, forget about us. Burn the letters I wrote to you.
Tottenham Burn my French letters?! Good God no! I intend to cherish their contents for years to come.
Anne Oh Totty...
Tottenham Come with me to England, my love. Be the French Dressing to my Beef On The Bone.
Anne Your Grace, there can be no future in this! I am Queen of France! You are prime minister of England!
Tottenham I don't give a fig for all that—it's you that I want, dammit!
Anne But consider. With me by the King's side counselling friendship to England, our two countries will forever be at peace. If I were to run away with you, Louis would be putty in the hands of Richeleeugh. War would be inevitable.

Tottenham gnaws at his stiff upper lip momentarily

Tottenham You are right. England must come first. Business before pleasure and all that.
Anne You know it makes sense.
Tottenham By God, Anne, but I love you.
Anne And I love you too—Hotspur.
Tottenham Then do one thing for me.
Anne Anything.
Tottenham Let me have some trifle to remember you by.
Anne (*wide-eyed*) But Totty, we do not keep blancmange in our boudoir.
Tottenham Not that sort of trifle, you silly old thing! I mean a token—to remind me of our love, when I am alone, in the cold hours before dawn.
Anne Constant. Fetch the walnut-inlaid box from my dressing table.

Constant goes off and returns moments later carrying a small wooden box

Anne takes it and passes it to Tottenham

Act I, Scene 10   33

There, My Lord. No Queen ever bestowed a more royal gift.
Tottenham Crikey! Not a jar of rough-cut marmalade, is it?
Anne No, My Lord... (*She places the box on an occasional table and carefully lifts the lid*) It is the True Quiche of Lorraine.

A faint green glow emanates from the box. Distant sepulchral chords are heard

Constant Majesty! You cannot! This is the most sacred gastronomic relic of all France!
Tottenham Good God, Anne! What the devil is it?
Anne It is legend, My Lord. The True Quiche was baked by St Denis of Lorraine, to fortify the body and spirit of the Frankish Emperor Charlemagne, on the eve of the Battle of Roncesvalles. But Charlemagne drew his sword, Flambérge, and smote the Quiche asunder. One half he sent to his Queen, the other he vowed to devour only once the Moors were driven from the sacred soil of France. The next day he rode out to join battle with the True Quiche before him. Thus inspired, his army vanquished the Moors—but Charlemagne fell upon the field of Roncesvalles.
Tottenham Good grief...
Anne Since the age of Charlemagne, the True Quiche has been given by the King of France, as a token of undying love when he takes a queen. One half of The Quiche is given to the Queen on her wedding night—the other is held for the King by the Cardinal of France, at the Carmelite Convent at Bèthune, where, legend has it, the True Quiche was first baked.
Tottenham I can't take this!
Anne You must.
Tottenham But what if you need it?
Anne Never fear, my love. The Quiche is never made whole, until either the Queen or King dies. In either case, it will hardly matter any more—will it?
Constant Majesty! This could place you in great jeopardy. The penalty for losing either portion of the True Quiche of Lorraine is——
Anne (*interrupting her*) No, Constant! I don't want to hear. Take it, my lord. It is a sacred token of undying love, and if my heart speaks true—it is rightfully yours.
Tottenham Oh Annie!
Anne Perhaps one day, Your Grace, when the years have eased your passion, you will feel able to return The Quiche to me—and I will know that our love is truly at an end.
Tottenham (*fiercely*) Never! Never, old girl!
Anne But until then, keep it close to your heart, and think of me.
Tottenham I shall! Dash it all—I shall! Every night I shall take out this box, gaze upon this piece of marvellous sloppy tart, and think of you.
Anne I know you will. Now—begone, my love! Whilst you still can. The

Cardinal's ravens haunt every tower and rooftop. Take care, my dearest Totty.

Constant Come, Your Grace, we shall take the secret passageway to my house, and thence, I will see you safely out of the City, and on to the road to Calais.

Anne Thank you, Constant. You are a true friend. (*She turns to Tottenham*)

Romantic music swells to an unbearable crescendo

Well, My Lord. This is au revoir...
Tottenham (*passionately*) Farewell, my lush Fields of France.
Anne (*likewise*) Adieu—my mighty Heart of England.

They embrace

Tottenham turns manfully away and follows Constant from the room

The Queen produces a handkerchief, and snivels softly into it. Music abates. Not a dry eye in the house

Lights down

Scene 11

The Courtyard of Monsieur Hoh-hi-hon's house

The Dame and Hoh-hi-hon enter

Hoh-hi-hon Entrez! Entrez! Welcome to Chez Hoh-hi-hon. This is the courtyard...
Dame Never mind the courtyard—where's the blinkin' pantry? I'm ruddy famished.

There is a sudden hammering on the door. Pus-sac's voice is heard

Pus-sac (*off*) Open up! In the name of the Cardinal!
Hoh-hi-hon Morbleu! The Guards!
Pus-sac Open this door, or we'll knock it down.
Dame Blimey! I'd have been better off kipping in the gutter. Well, go on then, let them in.

Hoh-hi-hon opens the door and Pus-sac and two Cardinal's Guards push their way in

Act I, Scene 11

Pus-sac Henri Hubért Hoh-hi-hon?
Hoh-hi-hon No. (*He points at the Dame*) She is.
Pus-sac (*ignoring him*) I have a warrant for your arrest on charges of high treason.
Hoh-hi-hon (*squeaking in terror*) High treason! But I've done nothing!
Pus-sac You are not obliged to say anything, but I must warn you that you will have no option but to spill your guts when we get you to the torture chamber!
Hoh-hi-hon The torture chamber?! No! Mercy! There's been some terrible mistake.
Pus-sac No mistake. Come on. You're coming with us.
Dame Yes, go on. Off you go. Don't you worry about me, I'll soon make meself at home. You couldn't just point me towards the larder before they take you off to the torture chamber, could you?
Pus-sac Who's this?
Hoh-hi-hon (*moaning*) I don't know.
Pus-sac Ha! You're full of French polish, aren't you?!
Hoh-hi-hon No! Honestly! I never saw her before in my life until tonight.
Pus-sac Don't give me that. (*To the Guards*) This must be the wife. Not quite the looker she's cracked up to be, is she?

They all laugh raucously

Dame How dare you?!
Pus-sac All right. We'd better take her in too.
Dame Take me in! What for?!

Pus-sac considers for a moment

Pus-sac Fouling the footway. Come on, you repulsive lump of dung!
Dame Gerroff! Unhand me, you coarse-cut Toulouse Sausage!

Amidst much scuffling and complaining, the Dame and Hoh-hi-hon are bundled off

A few seconds later, Plonquer leads D'Artagnan on from the other side of the stage

D'Artagnan Is this the place?
Plonquer This is it. Not bad, eh?
D'Artagnan Well, it's not exactly the Paris Ritz, is it?
Plonquer Well, you wouldn't want to find yourself staying in a room between Neil Hamilton and Jonathan Aitken, would you?

D'Artagnan True. (*He cocks an ear*) Hey! Wait. Someone's coming.
Plonquer That'll be Hoh-hi-hon.
D'Artagnan No, it won't. Not unless he usually creeps into his own house like a thief in the night.
Plonquer Oh, heck! What shall we do?
D'Artagnan What shall we do? Apprehend the intruder, naturally.
Plonquer (*to the audience*) Naturally.
D'Artagnan Stand by.

The door slowly opens. D'Artagnan leaps forward, and drags the newcomer through the doorway by the scruff of the neck

Got you! You sneaking cockroach!
Constant (*for it is she*) Merde!
D'Artagnan Morbleu! It's a girl!
Constant Release me, you ruffian!
D'Artagnan My apologies, Mademoiselle. Now, who are you?
Constant I am Constant Hoh-hi-hon. And this is my house! So more to the point, sir—who are you?!
D'Artagnan Me? I'm your new lodger.
Constant My lodger?! I don't have a lodger. And who is this?
D'Artagnan Plonquer. My valet.
Plonquer How do.
Constant (*ignoring him*) I take it this is some arrangement on the part of my foolish husband? Where is he?
D'Artagnan Out.
Constant I see. (*To D'Artagnan*) Why are you staring at me?
D'Artagnan Because you're so perfect.
Constant Monsieur!
D'Artagnan No. It's true. I swear I never saw such beauty before.
Constant I think you'd better go.
D'Artagnan (*fiercely*) Never! I'd rather lose my sword arm than leave your side.
Constant (*fascinated*) Who are you?
D'Artagnan D'Artagnan. Son of D'Artagnan. Sprung from the sun-warmed earth of Gascony to melt your heart of ice.
Constant Mon Dieu! But you have a silver tongue for a country lad.
D'Artagnan We country lads never do thing by halves.
Constant I'll bet.
D'Artagnan We have an insatiable lust for life, you know.
Constant So I've heard.
D'Artagnan I could show you sometime.
Constant I think I might like that.
D'Artagnan (*without looking at him*) Shove off, Plonquer.

Act I, Scene 11   37

Plonquer Certainly, sir. Shoving off now, sir. (*To the audience*) Fast worker, isn't he?!

Plonquer ambles off

D'Artagnan You were saying...
Constant I was saying... (*She catches herself*) No! I'm sorry—this is madness! I don't have time for this. I have someone extremely important waiting for me outside. There are dangerous games afoot this night.
D'Artagnan (*slapping his thigh*) Ha! Dangerous games are my stock-in-trade!
Constant No, D'Artagnan! You must not get involved. You are just a boy.
D'Artagnan Now I am a boy. But soon, Lady, I shall be a Musketeer. And my only duty shall be to die for my King.
Constant Surely not.
D'Artagnan To die, Lady... When France has need of my blood.
Constant Until then—stay alive. For me. (*She turns to go*)
D'Artagnan Constant...
Constant What?
D'Artagnan I'm in love with you.
Constant C'est impossible!
D'Artagnan Maybe so. But I am.
Constant You cannot! You must not... Now, I beg you—wait here!

Constant sweeps out

D'Artagnan (*to himself*) Wait here?! With dangerous games afoot, and the girl that I love in mortal peril?! Never! (*He catches himself*) Hup! Learn to control your recklessness, D'Artagnan! First things first. Fetch help. Find the Three Musketeers!

D'Artagnan exits L

A second later, Plonquer enters R, Athos following

Plonquer Hey, Monsieur D! Look who I found propping up a bar round the corner! Says he's a friend of yours.
Athos (*calling*) D'Artagnan?
Plonquer That's odd... He must have gone out again.

Constant sweeps back on, now followed by the Duke of Tottenham

Constant Where is D'Artagnan?
Plonquer Search me.

Constant Not without rubber gloves. (*To Athos*) And who are you?
Athos I am Athos. Of the Musketeers. And you are Madame Hoh-hi-hon, are you not?
Constant I might be...
Athos You are—I recognize you from Court. (*Narrowly*) But I do not know this gentleman.
Constant He is a guest of her Majesty.
Athos Really?
Constant Really. (*She comes to a decision*) If you are a Musketeer, sir, then I must ask you to assist me in a matter of the utmost importance to the throne of France.
Athos Which is?
Constant This gentleman urgently requires an escort out of the City.
Athos Why?
Constant Because the Cardinal's Guards seek him in every alley and cellar in Paris.
Athos Why?
Constant Never mind. His Grace must achieve Calais by dawn, to take ship for England.
Athos His Grace?
Constant All right. It seems I have little choice but to trust you. This is the Duke of Tottenham.
Athos I see... (*Stiffly*) I am a King's Musketeer, Madame. Not nursemaid to wayward Englishmen.

Pus-sac and four Guards tumble on

Pus-sac Hey! You there!
Constant The Cardinal's Guards!
Tottenham Oh, cripes!
Plonquer Oh, no. This can't be happening to me.
Athos Go, Plonquer! Fetch Aramis and Porthos—and find D'Artagnan!
Plonquer (*grovelling*) Oh, thank you! Thank you! Thank you so much!

Plonquer turns tail and flees

Constant Monsieur, you have to get his Grace away—for the Queen's sake!
Athos I take orders from the King, Madame. And nobody else.
Constant For the Queen, Monsieur!
Athos The man that tries to give me orders, is asking for trouble.
Pus-sac Hey. Cloth-ears!
Athos I'd have to kill him.
Pus-sac (*bellowing*) You! You drunken slackwit! I command you to arrest that English dog!

Act I, Scene 11   39

Athos smiles his most dangerous smile

Athos He had to go and say it, didn't he. (*He turns to Tottenham*) Fortune smiles on you this night, Your Grace. Your withdrawal shall be covered by the finest sword in Paris.
Tottenham I say, that's awfully decent of you. Next time you're in Whitehall, do pop in for a cuppa, won't you?
Athos Just go, Englishman.
Pus-sac Arrest him, you cretin!
Tottenham Cheerio then. (*He bows to Constant*) Madame.

Tottenham turns on his heel and melts into the night

Athos And you Madame Hoh-hi-hon.
Constant I cannot. I have to warn the Queen.
Pus-sac You've let him escape, you idiot!
Athos Go, Madame!
Constant No!
Pus-sac Very well, Musketeer—it is now you who are under arrest!
Athos Come and take me—if you dare. Who is first to die upon the blade of Athos?!

Sinister music

The Guards part to allow Roquefort through, a cloak draped over his arm

Roquefort So, the goose has flown—and only little worms remain. Six to one, Monsieur Athos? I think even you would find those odds a little … overwhelming.
Athos I'm willing to try, Roquefort—are you?
Roquefort Dear me, no—not when I have recourse to a pistol. (*He throws back his cloak to reveal a gleaming wheel-lock pistol*) I take it that even your charmed hide cannot turn a pistol ball, Musketeer?
Athos You despicable coward.
Roquefort (*pleasantly*) You'll be sorry you said that. Now, lower your guard if you please, Monsieur.
Athos Never. You may shoot me. I choose death above dishonour.
Roquefort How very melodramatic of you. Unfortunately, my shot is reserved for the lady—unless you surrender your weapon.

Athos knows he is beaten. He elegantly reverse flips his rapier, to present the hilt to Roquefort

Athos You are a villain, Roquefort.

Roquefort I know. A pantomime villain. (*He takes the sword*) All right... Remove these traitors to the Bastille—and do it quickly. No-one must know they are there. (*He seizes Constant by the arm and hisses into her ear*) It's going to be our little secret. Ha ha ha ha!!

Audience participation as Roquefort and the Guards bundle their prisoners off

A moment later, D'Artagnan runs on, with Aramis, Porthos, and Plonquer following

D'Artagnan Constant!
Plonquer Too late!
D'Artagnan After them!
Aramis (*catching him back*) No, D'Artagnan! Unless you would risk the lives of Athos and the lady.
D'Artagnan But they have taken the woman I love!
Porthos Fear not, lad. Tottenham is long gone, and without the Englishman, they can't prove a thing against Madame Hoh-hi-hon, or the Queen.
Plonquer And as your new lady friend is the Queen's favourite...
Aramis ...The Cardinal dare not harm one hair of her head.
D'Artagnan (*taking heart*) You are right! And Athos, of course, will withstand the most fiendish and ingenious torture.
Aramis Er, no, Athos will crack at the first whiff of a glass of burgundy.
Porthos Which is why we are going to break into the Bastille to rescue him.
D'Artagnan We are?
Porthos We are.
Plonquer (*horrified*) We are?
Aramis We are.
D'Artagnan (*elated*) We are!
Plonquer (*aside*) I'm not.
Aramis We are, after all...
All All for one, and one for all!

Song 4

Followed by Lights down and——

—Curtain

ENTR'ACTE

ACT II

Scene 1

A dungeon beneath the infamous Bastille prison

Athos and Constant are comprehensively strapped down on a pair of mortuary-style slabs

Athos Courage, Madame.
Constant I am vastly comforted by your presence, Monsieur.
Athos We shall defy them together.
Constant Yes. And die together.
Athos Yes... Well... Let's not get carried away. (*Peering around*) Mon Dieu! I could murder a pint.

Roquefort enters, followed by two shuffling, hooded figures (Zoot and Zach)

Roquefort Ah... Madame Hoh-hi-hon. Monsieur Athos. I would say make yourselves comfortable—but I fear it is an impossibility. Ha ha ha ha!! Allow me to introduce our resident torturers: Messieurs Pinch and Tweak...

One of the figures pulls up its hood

Zoot Er... no, it's us actually...
Roquefort (*recoiling*) Zut Alors!
Zoot Oui! C'est moi!

The other figure whips off his hood

Zach That's right! And me—Zach Rebleur!
Roquefort I know who you are!
Zoot You do?
Roquefort Yes. The two most incompetent buffoons in the entire Cardinal's Guard! Where are the torturers?
Zach They just popped out—for a little pain.

Drum roll—Boom Boom

(*Coming down to the audience*) Pain! Torturers! Geddit?! It's by way of being a French joke. (*He explains*) Pain is French for bread, see... Oh, forget it.

Roquefort All right. We've wasted enough time. To business. (*To Constant*) Now Madame, what do you have to say for yourself?

Constant Nothing.

Roquefort Oh, come come. That really isn't the attitude. You see you are already lost. Down here, you're not a person any more. You might as well be on the meat counter at Tesco [or other local supermarket]. Down here, on the slabs, you're just so much offal to be disposed of. So, why don't you just tell me what you know, eh? Then we can all go back upstairs for a glass of chilled chablis and a vol-au-vent. Very civilised.

Constant I know nothing that could possibly interest you, Monsieur.

Roquefort Oh, goody. You're going to be stubborn, aren't you?

Athos Hey! I could use a drink. Haven't you got a bottle of decent claret in this cellar?

Roquefort You would be well advised to save your breath for screaming, Monsieur.

Athos How about a cognac?

Roquefort (*smiling grimly*) I think we'd better get to work.

Athos No ice.

Roquefort All right, boots off.

Zach Right away, Your Grace.

Zach and Zoot start to remove their boots

Roquefort Not you, you cretins! The prisoners.

Zach Oh, right. (*To Zoot*) Thought it was a bit informal.

They tug off the prisoners' boots

Constant Oh!

Roquefort Ah, yes, it is rather chill below ground, is it not? But fear not, Madame—your dainty extremities will soon be warm enough. (*Flipping out a hand to Zach*) Matches.

Zach (*producing a box*) Paris Matches?

Roquefort Ideal.

Constant You are lighting a fire, Monsieur?

Roquefort Exactly so. Observé. First, we insert the incendiaries betwixt the helpless pinkies, thus.

Constant Oh no!

Roquefort Next, as they say in Angleterre... (*In an appalling Mary Poppins accent*) "Stroik a light!" (*He strikes a match on Zoot's head*) Then—Voila! Feet of Flames! Ha ha ha ha!! (*He stoops to ignite the matches*)

Act II, Scene 1   43

Zoot STOP!
Roquefort What?
Zoot You can't do that.
Roquefort (*icily*) And why not?
Zoot This is 1625. Matches haven't been invented yet.
Roquefort Merde! A flaw in my fiendish plan! (*He blows out the match, and retires cursing to the back of the dungeon*)
Zach (*aside*) What did you go and tell him that for?
Zoot (*aside*) 'Cos I deplore the use of torture as an instrument of state repression.
Zach (*amazed*) You do?
Zoot Certainly. I am a member of Amnesia International.
Zach (*impressed*) Really? What's that then?

Pause

Zoot (*puzzled*) I've forgotten.
Roquefort (*coming back downstage*) Very well. Thumbscrews, I think.
Zach Thumbscrews. Right away. Thumbscrews. (*He turns to rummage in a box of implements*) Got it!
Roquefort What's that?
Zach That's a thumbscrew, that is.
Roquefort That's a corkscrew, you moron.
Zach (*astonished*) Is it? Well, that'll come in handy, then.
Roquefort For what?
Zach For opening his claret.
Roquefort He isn't having claret, you numbskull! Take it back to the kitchen.
Zach But I'll miss the fun.
Roquefort (*shouting*) You're not here to enjoy yourself!!

Zach mooches out

I, on the other hand, am. Ha ha ha ha!!

Audience participation

(*To the audience*) All right. Pipe down! (*He turns back to the prisoners*) Time to introduce you to a fellow resident of this particular dungeon. Unlike you two—who will, I fear, have but a few hours in which to enjoy the less than extensive facilities—my little playmate lives here all the time. Why don't I ask him to—drop in. (*He peers up towards the ceiling, and calls*) Oh Monsieur Scuttle... Come on down!!

Sinister music as a huge, bright green, furry spider begins to descend on a line from overhead. Constant squirms in alarm

Constant Oh! Monsieur Athos! Regardez!
Athos Stay calm, Madame.
Roquefort Whatever is the matter? Don't you like—SPIDERS?! Ha ha ha ha!! Oh, but this one is perfectly house trained. I call him "Le Scuttle".
Constant (*horrified*) Le Scuttle?
Roquefort Precisely—the fastest and most convenient way to get to a confession! Ha ha ha ha ha!!
Constant Please! Don't let it near me!
Roquefort Near you? (*With mock concern*) My dear girl. Of course I won't let it near you. Dear me, no—not near you... ON YOU!! Ha ha ha ha!!
Constant (*struggling*) You fiend!
Roquefort Tell me what I want to know!
Athos Constant! Remember your Queen!
Constant (*weeping*) I do, I do.
Roquefort Tell me!
Athos Be strong, Constant!
Roquefort Confess!
Constant Never.
Roquefort You'll talk.
Constant No! (*With sudden icy composure*) No, Your Grace—I will not.
Roquefort (*furiously*) Then suffer the consequences!

Le Scuttle has now descended to a few inches above Constant's heaving, er ... diaphragm. Roquefort produces a large pair of pantomime scissors which he holds to the spider's thread

(*To the audience*) Shall I? Shall I?

Audience participation. But Roquefort snips anyway

Ooops! Clumsy moi! Ha ha ha ha!!

The spider drops—apparently behind the slab

Constant Oh! Where is it?! Where's it gone?!
Roquefort (*enjoying himself*) IT'S BEHIND YOU!

Le Scuttle (now a glove puppet duplicate operated by a puppeteer hidden behind the slab) reappears. Constant shrieks as the hideous arachnid commences its laborious climb along the length of her frozen body

Act II, Scene 1   45

Just let me know when you're ready to tell me something...

Constant emits a small squeak of abject terror

(*Filing his nails*) Suit yourself ... better make sure you speak before it gets as far as your mouth though. Once it's crawling across your face, dragging its fat, hairy abdomen behind it, you won't feel much like chatting.

Zoot (*idly*) I knew a woman like that once.
Roquefort Didn't chat much?
Zoot No... Fat, hairy abdomen.
Constant (*desperately*) Monsieur, please!! I beg you!

Zach enters

Spotting the spider, he seizes up a shovel propped against the wall

Zach It's all right! I'll get it!
Roquefort What are you doing?

Quick as a flash, Zach scoops the giant spider off Constant, tosses it up into the air, and as it lands, whacks it with the back of the shovel

Zach Have you ever seen one as big as that before, eh?! Ooh la la!
Roquefort (*in stunned disbelief*) What are you doing?
Zach Ugly little brute.
Roquefort (*bellowing*) What are you doing?!
Zach Didn't you see it? It was a bloomin' great spider—a whopper.
Roquefort (*numbly*) That was church property, that spider.
Zach Sorry. Can't abide them. Give me the collywobbles they do.
Roquefort (*picking up the squished spider tenderly*) And a family pet!
Zach Nasty, hairy, little spook.
Roquefort That was my very best instrument of coercion, that spider ... one hundred per cent success rate with the ladies!
Zach (*to Athos*) They come from another planet, you know.
Roquefort (*raging*) And you've just squished it!!

The cell door swings open, and Richeleeugh enters

Richeleeugh Well—anything?
Roquefort (*tossing the remains of Le Scuttle over his shoulder*) They won't talk.
Athos (*interrupting*) Excuse me. I'd like to talk—about the lack of refreshments in this sewer.

Richeleeugh (*ignoring Athos*) Then we must employ sterner measures.
Athos Hey, your effluence! Break out the communion wine, will you?
Richeleeugh I begin to tire of this drunkard's voice, Roquefort. The mask, I think.
Athos Oh, no. Wait.
Roquefort (*grinning evilly*) Yes, your eminence. (*To Zoot*) The mask!
Zoot Oooh. Mask! Yes. Got one of them. Hang about. (*He goes to rummage in the box again and produces a Bart Simpson mask*)
Athos No. Please. Not the mask.
Richeleeugh I am afraid so.
Zoot Here we go.
Richeleeugh Proceed.
Athos No. NO. NOOO!! AAAAAARGGGHMMMFFF...FF...F...

A brief, frantic, desperate struggle ensues as Athos is held down and fitted with the mask

Zach (*stepping back and dusting off his hands*) Done it.
Richeleeugh Let me see...

The Cardinal peers at the recumbent Athos, then straightens up, and turns to Zach

Tell me, Rebleur...
Zach Yes, your eminence?
Richeleeugh Have you heard of that famous novel by Monsieur Dumas: "The Man in the Bart Simpson Mask"?
Zach Can't say as I have, your eminence.
Richeleeugh No. Nor have I. (*He grabs Athos by the collar and pulls him upright*)

The Musketeer's head is now encased in a rubber Bart Simpson mask

(*Screaming*) GET IT OFF HIM!!

As Zach and Zoot struggle to free Athos from the Bart Simpson mask, Richeleeugh crosses to look down on Constant. He feigns surprise

But wait! Surely this is Madame Hoh-hi-hon, the Queen's wardrobe mistress?
Roquefort (*puzzled*) Yes, your eminence.
Richeleeugh Then I fear there has been some terrible mistake. Release this lady at once!

Act II, Scene 1   47

Roquefort But, your eminence...
Richeleeugh DO AS I SAY, ROQUEFORT!

Roquefort signals to Zoot and Zach, who proceed to unstrap Constant from the slab. Richeleeugh pulls Roquefort to one side

    (*Sotto voce*) There's more than one way to skin a cat, you know, Roquefort. Little does she know we have her husband in the cell next door. (*He turns back to Constant*)

Constant is now standing, rubbing at her freed wrists

    My sincerest apologies, Madame, if my servants have inconvenienced you in any way... I assure you, it is a misunderstanding, nothing more.
Constant Thank you, your eminence. I am quite unharmed.
Richeleeugh All is well, then. Roquefort—would you be so good as to escort this lady back to the world of daylight?
Roquefort Of course, your eminence. (*He goes to lead Constant out*)

She breaks free from him

Constant Your eminence! I beg you! Let me plead clemency for this gentleman also. His only fault was to come to my defence.
Richeleeugh Alas my child, I fear that is not the only fault of this renegade. I must tell you that Monsieur Athos has many sins to atone for. And this is a place of atonement.

Pus-sac enters the dungeon

Pus-sac Your pardon, eminence. (*He whispers in the Cardinal's ear*)
Richeleeugh Thank you, Captain. Ask them to come in, would you... (*He turns to Athos*) Well, since you have been so foolish as to hold your tongue despite the attentions of my minions, I regret you leave me no alternative but to hand this matter over to an altogether less enlightened authority. (*He signals to Pus-sac*)

Pus-sac opens the dungeon door to admit two red-robed and hooded figures

    These brothers are agents of the Holy Inquisition. From Rome. I think you will find they are rather more expert in the art of... persuasion. I commend you to their tender care, confident that you will soon wish to God that you had told me all you know. Ha ha ha ha!!

Audience participation as Richeleeugh sweeps out, followed by Pus-sac, Zoot A Lor, and Zach Rebleur

Roquefort waits for Constant, who lingers in the dungeon doorway as Athos regards the Inquisitors with a curl of his lip

Athos Well, my friends. Do your worst. It'll take more than a couple of Italian sickos in pointy hats to break a King's Musketeer.

Unperturbed, one of the hooded figures slowly raises a bony finger to his lips in a sinister "shhh" gesture, as the other moves to stand behind Athos

Well, what are you waiting for, you sorry vultures?

Sudden, terrifying, organ music, as the Inquisitor behind Athos raises both hands over his head. He holds aloft a hideous iron mask covered in rivets and odd protrusions

(*Craning his neck*) What are you doing back there?
Constant (*muttering in horror*) Merciful God in Heaven.
Roquefort Come, lady.

Roquefort pulls Constant out after him, banging the cell door shut behind him

Athos (*managing to look over his shoulder*) No... NO! Not the iron mask!!

The first figure lays hold of Athos to hold him steady whilst the second lowers the hideous contraption on to his head

(*Bellowing*) NO!!

The mask begins to swing shut

(*Screaming*) NOOOOOOOOOOOOOOOOOOOO...

With a sickening metallic click, his scream is suddenly cut off

Black-out

Scene 2

The throne room of Richeleeugh

Roquefort enters, leading the Dame, and Hoh-hi-hon, Pus-sac, Zach and Zoot following

Roquefort This way, you fortunate scum. The Cardinal has granted you an audience.
Dame No, thanks. I've already got one. That's all those people asleep down there.
Roquefort Do you know who I am?
Dame Why—can't you remember?
Roquefort I am Le Chevalier Du Lobster Roquefort.
Dame You can be Le Duc Du Crabstix Cocktail for all I care. Excuse me, are you in charge of these dilberts?
Richeleeugh Do you know who I am?
Dame We've just done that one. It wasn't funny the first time.
Richeleeugh I am Richeleeugh.
Dame (*aside*) Rich fruitcake.
Richeleeugh (*intoning*) I sit at the King's right hand.
Dame (*also intoning*) And prevent him from picking his nose.
Richeleeugh And you are?
Dame Desirée.
Richeleeugh How singularly inappropriate.
Dame Whatcha mean?!
Richeleeugh Well, let's just say, I assume you were not named Desirée for your allure.
Dame No—it's because my face resembles a large, pink, knobbly spud.
Richeleeugh I thought as much. Listen well, Madame Desirée—I am a seeker after knowledge.
Dame That's nice.
Richeleeugh And?
Dame And what?
Richeleeugh What do you know?
Dame About what?
Richeleeugh Anything.
Dame Anything?
Richeleeugh Anything.
Dame Nothing.
Richeleeugh Just as I thought. All right. Throw her in the Seine.
Dame In the Seine? Now hang on a minute.
Richeleeugh Next.

Dame I'll tell you what! You're the insane one, pal!
Pus-sac Come on, you.
Richeleeugh And make sure she doesn't float.
Dame You're nuttier than nougat, mate!
Richeleeugh I can't abide floaters.
Dame (*shouting*) I'd rather be a floater than a dingleberry!

Zach and Zoot drag the Dame out

Richeleeugh turns to regard Hoh-hi-hon with his lizard's gaze

Hoh-hi-hon (*with a terrified giggle*) She's a one, isn't she…?
Richeleeugh (*sighing*) Monsieur Hoh-hi-hon. What am I to do with you?
Hoh-hi-hon Er… Let me go?
Richeleeugh I don't think so.
Hoh-hi-hon Be nice?
Richeleeugh Alas… It's not in my nature.
Hoh-hi-hon (*collapsing*) But I'm innocent, I tell you! I have nothing but respect for the law!
Richeleeugh Ah, but my dear Hoh-hi-hon, you are known to associate with certain disreputable characters who do not share your exacting moral standards.
Hoh-hi-hon My snails, you mean?
Richeleeugh Not your snails.
Hoh-hi-hon The wife! Dear God! I told her. Don't get involved in politics I said! Stay out of it! But she won't. She has such an opinion of herself, your eminence. There's no telling her.
Richeleeugh You two don't get on?
Hoh-hi-hon Not only that—we don't get off. Oh, it was all the King's idea! A marriage of convenience he said. His Snail Factor with Her Wardrobe Mistress. Convenient? Huh! It's turned out to be most inconvenient. She doesn't like my snails, and worse still, she doesn't like me!
Richeleeugh As it happens, your dear lady wife was also taken into custody tonight, in connection with certain other matters. She was questioned, naturally—but I fear she did not reveal herself fully.
Hoh-hi-hon (*gloomily*) No. She won't do that for me either.
Richeleeugh I mean, you repulsive old scrag-end, that she did not admit all that she knows.
Hoh-hi-hon Oh, she wouldn't—she's horribly stubborn.
Richeleeugh Whereas you, by careful observation of her movements, may well be able to throw some light on what is going on.
Hoh-hi-hon Going on? Yes! That's it! Something's going on. She's a very naughty girl, you know.

Richeleeugh She must be punished.
Hoh-hi-hon Yes! Yes! Punished severely.
Richeleeugh I agree. That's settled then. So you'll spy on your own wife for me?
Hoh-hi-hon Eh?
Richeleeugh Ah. No. I agree. It's asking too much of a man.
Hoh-hi-hon No! No! It isn't!
Richeleeugh Perhaps it would be best if you just went straight to the torture chamber.
Hoh-hi-hon No! Let me spy for you! Please! I beg you! I'll do it! I'll give you Constant on a plate!
Richeleeugh Oh, no... Forget I mentioned it. It was a foolish thought.
Hoh-hi-hon No! It wasn't!
Richeleeugh Oh, yes, it was.
Hoh-hi-hon Oh, no, it wasn't! Please! I promise you! Give me one more chance! (*Blubbing*) Just one teensy little chance.
Richeleeugh But how do I know you will keep your word?
Hoh-hi-hon Oh, I will. I Promise you!
Richeleeugh Very well. Stop snivelling. You have twenty-four hours to bring me something useful.
Hoh-hi-hon Yes! I will! You just see if I don't! You won't be sorry! Bless you, your eminence. Bless you!
Richeleeugh Pus-sac. Show this despicable old croque-monsieur the back door.

Pus-sac leads Hoh-hi-hon out

Now let the mischief work! Ha ha ha ha ha!!

Audience participation. Lights down

Scene 3

The banks of the Seine

The Dame is led on by Zach and Zoot

Zach Well, here we are. The river bank.
Dame I can't believe you're going to go through with this.
Zoot Nor can I.
Zach Look. She's going into the river, and that's that.
Dame But I'll get Perrier up my derriere.

Zoot She's right, Zach. I don't like it.
Zach Look at it this way, Zoot. We're helping to restock the river. One more fat old trout gasping for air in the putrid waters of the Seine.
Zoot Oh come off it. The Seine is clogged up enough already, without lobbing in lardy old biddies from Gascony.
Dame Oi! Who are you calling an old biddy?! I'll have you know that I am a damson in distress! You two ought to be ashamed of yourselves!
Zach Oh, give it a rest, will you? We don't have a choice, all right?
Dame Stuff 'n' nonsense! Of course you do.
Zach Oh, yeah? We'll just let you slip, shall we? And what are we supposed to tell the Cardinal?
Dame Tell him to do his own dirty work.
Zach Ha! He'd marmelize us.
Dame Rubbish. You're just a couple of cringing lap-dogs, wagging your scrawny little bottoms every time His Nibs gives you another kicking.
Zach That's not true!
Dame Oh, yes, it is! Look at you—Yap! Yap! You're pathetic. (*To the audience*) Aren't they, boys and girls?!

Audience participation

Zach Oh, no, we're not.

Audience participation

Oh, no, we're not. Tell them, Zoot!
Zoot (*abruptly*) No. She's right! I'm fed up with being Richeleeugh's lap dancer.
Zach Lap dog.
Zoot Whatever! I'm sick of being devious, selfish, and double-dealing in the Cardinal's name! (*Declaiming*) I am a freeborn Frenchman, and demand the right to be devious, selfish, and double-dealing in my own right!
Dame Bravo! Quite right too!
Zoot Citizens! It is time to take to the barricades!
Zach Barricades?! Zoot! What are you doing?!
Zoot (*gnomically*) When the pilchards follow the trawler, it is because they know that the seagulls can't snorkel.
Zach WHAT??
Dame The revolution starts here!
Zoot Too right it does!
Zach But it can't! You're one hundred and seventy years too early!
Dame Who cares?! (*She strikes a pose like the Delacrois Liberty*) Pour la gloire!
Zoot Liberté!

Act II, Scene 3   53

Dame Fraternité!
Zoot Mediocrité!
Dame Senilité!
Zach That's not until seventeen eighty-nine!
Dame We shall sing the national anthem!
Zach No!
Dame & Zoot A Frenchman went to the lavatory for to have a jolly good
                    poo!
          He took his coat and trousers off, and he sat down on the loo...
          But when he reached out for the paper,
          He found that someone had been there before!
          Ou est, le papier?! Ou est, le papier?!
          Marche on! Marche on! With poo on your bum!
          Ou est, le papier?!
Dame (*to the audience*) Come on everybody! Let's have some young citizen-volunteers up on stage here, to join in the patriotic singing! Who'd like to become French revolutionaries?!

They descend into the audience, round up some volunteers, and then sing the song twice more with full accompaniment, and a set of actions which are best left to the imagination for the time being

Song 5

Following the song, distribution of bon-bons, applause, etc., the Dame makes her exit whilst the going is good

   Au revoir, citizens! Vive La Republique!

The Dame goes off

Zach Well, you've really gone and done it this time, haven't you?
Zoot I don't care! We are turning over a new worm.
Zach We are?
Zoot Yes! No more dirty work. No more wiggling our little bottoms like lap dancers.
Zach What are we going to do instead?
Zoot We are going to put right some of the rotten things we've done.
Zach Starting when?
Zoot Right now. Come on!

   Zach and Zoot exit

Lights down

Scene 4

The house of Monsieur Hoh-hi-hon

D'Artagnan is slumped in a chair

The door creaks open, and Constant enters

D'Artagnan leaps up

D'Artagnan Constant! Oh, Constant! Thank Heavens you are safe!
Constant Safe for the moment. But Richeleeugh grows bolder with each day that passes. Where is that loathsome old snake, my husband?
D'Artagnan Monsieur Hoh-hi-hon returned but half an hour ago, and straightway retired for the night. He seemed somewhat distracted. But how did you escape?
Constant His eminence released me. Claimed my arrest was an error. But he is planning something—I know it.
D'Artagnan And Athos?
Constant Oh, it was horrible, D'Artagnan, horrible! They locked that brave gentleman's noble head into a hideous mask of iron, that he may neither see nor hear, eat nor drink—only suffer.
D'Artagnan Poor Athos—he will be suffering indeed if he is unable to pour a cognac down his throat.
Constant I fear he will be driven quite mad.
D'Artagnan He will not be there long enough. My sworn companions, Porthos and Aramis, are even now on their way to liberate him.
Constant Can two men storm the Bastille? They are mad!
D'Artagnan No—they are Musketeers. I should have accompanied them, but I hoped against hope that the Queen would intervene on your behalf, and determined to wait for you here.
Constant The Queen knew nothing of my predicament. You may be sure that Richeleeugh kept it from her.
D'Artagnan Well, you are safe now.
Constant Alas, I can never be safe again. I am too close to Her Majesty. My life is in perpetual danger.
D'Artagnan No, my love, not while this son of Gascony lives to defend you.
Constant No, D'Artagnan—I am cursed to die. Shun me. Spurn me. Live for yourself.
D'Artagnan Never! If I cannot live for you, I would rather not live at all!
Constant Why, D'Artagnan, why?!
D'Artagnan I love you.
Constant You cannot.

Act II, Scene 4   55

D'Artagnan I do.
Constant But I am a married woman.
D'Artagnan That doesn't matter. We're French!
Constant Oh, D'Artagnan…
D'Artagnan Oh, Constant…

Song 6

The song is followed by a tender kiss

That is the first time I have ever seen you smile. Are you happy, Constant?
Constant Happy? Oh, D'Artagnan—can one be truly happy, knowing so many dark secrets?
D'Artagnan I don't know. What do you mean?
Constant I cannot tell you. You are pledged to the King.
D'Artagnan Constant. My life belongs to the King. My soul is pledged to you.
Constant Very well. My mistress, the Queen, has done something unbelievably foolhardy. She has ended a wild and ill-conceived *amour* with the Duke of Tottenham, but has sent him home to England bearing a secret memento of their affair!
D'Artagnan What?
Constant The True Quiche of Lorraine!
D'Artagnan Sacré Camembért!
Constant Exactement! You see why I am sick with worry? I am sure that evil must come of it.
D'Artagnan Not necessarily. One man, armed only with his ingenuity and a rapier, and sustained by an immense bag of pork scratchings, could journey to England and effect its recovery. He would have to be reckless to a fault, of course. Probably a Gascon.
Constant You would do that—for the Queen?
D'Artagnan No, Constant. I would do it for you.
Constant No. It is too dangerous. Besides, what would it achieve? The Queen does not want the Quiche returned. She is innocent as a child, and perceives no danger. (*She shudders*) But she has not been inside the dungeons of the Bastille, for a personal consultation with Monsieur Scuttle!
D'Artagnan How you must have suffered, my love. Come, stay by my side. We shall find Porthos, Aramis, and with any luck—Athos, and then plan a course of wildly improbable action.
Constant No. I must to the Queen and tell her what has befallen. Will you escort me thither?
D'Artagnan I will not let you out of my sight, lady.

Constant and D'Artagnan kiss, and, slipping an arm around each other, they exit

After a moment, Monsieur Hoh-hi-hon emerges from hiding

Hoh-hi-hon So, the True Quiche of Lorraine, eh? Very interesting. I'm sure his eminence will be most grateful for that little nugget. Ha! I'll teach you to warble slushy duets with my missus, you squealing Gascon runt! (*To the audience*) What will his eminence do once I've shared this information with him, d'you think? Tell you what... Let's find out, shall we? Hee hee hee hee!!

Audience participation as Hoh-hi-hon shuffles off, chuckling

Lights down then straight up on:

Scene 5

A room in the Louvre Palace

Louis and Richeleeugh enter

Louis A ball, Cardinal?
Richeleeugh In honour of your wedding anniversary, Majesty.
Louis Oh, yes, capital idea. Not like you to think of that. Never had you down as a party animal.
Richeleeugh Ah, Your Majesty, how well you know me. I must confess to an ulterior motive.
Louis (*sharply*) Eh? What do you mean?
Richeleeugh It cannot have escaped Your Majesty's attention that all Paris has been aflame with rumour surrounding the state of your marriage.
Louis Wumour? Concerning what, Siwwah?
Richeleeugh (*with a pained expression*) Concerning the Queen, Your Majesty.
Louis Indeed? And what, pway, is the thwust of this tittle-tattle?
Richeleeugh That the Queen has been—how to put it— (*he pauses*) playing away, Your Majesty.
Louis (*shouting*) Playing away?! MORT DE MA VIE!! How dare you, Wicheleeugh?! How dare you?! Scuwwilous scandalmongerwing, that is all. Malicious mudslinging!
Richeleeugh (*soothingly*) Obviously, Majesty. But nonetheless—mud sticks. This sort of thing is bad for the Monarchy. Bad for France. Best

nipped in the bud, I'm sure you'd agree. One feels that a gesture is called for.
Louis A gesture? What sort of gesture?
Richeleeugh An act of public reconciliation, between the Queen and youself.
Louis Ah! Like a ball, you mean.
Richeleeugh A ball, yes, but only as a stage for something more dramatic. A grand gesture, to silence speculation once and for all.
Louis Go on.
Richeleeugh (*eyes blazing*) The True Quiche of Lorraine. Reunite the halves.
Louis (*shocked*) But... But it's never been done!
Richeleeugh Be bold, Majesty! Fortune favours the brave.
Louis But the Quiche, Richeleeugh... We weally don't know...
Richeleeugh (*shouting*) You are King of France! The Quiche is yours! You can do with it as you please. (*Slyly*) Can't you...?
Louis What? Well, yes! Yes, of course we can.
Richeleeugh There you are then.
Louis Yes. Right. Well. That's settled then. The Quiche. Shall I order some more food, do you think, or will the Quiche be enough?
Richeleeugh (*patiently*) The Quiche may not be *eaten*, Majesty. It is an object of veneration. If either party should fail to produce their portion, the penalty is gruesome beyond contemplation.
Louis Perhaps a few sausage rolls, then.
Richeleeugh Leave all the arrangements to me.
Louis Good idea. I'll go and tell the Queen.
Richeleeugh I would dearly love to be there when you break the good news to Her Majesty.
Louis I'll bet you would, but you've got a knees-up to organise. So get on wiv it.
Richeleeugh Your Majesty...

Richeleeugh bows as Louis sweeps off

It will be my pleasure. Ha ha ha ha ha!! Ha ha ha ha ha!!

Audience participation

Scene 6

The Queen's boudoir

Anne and Constant enter

Anne Oh Constant! Thank Heavens you are here!

Constant What's wrong, Majesty?!

Anne The King has commanded a great banquet to mark our wedding anniversary. Louis has decreed that the pieces of the True Quiche of Lorraine be reunited!

Constant No!

Anne Yes!

Constant Morbleu! I sense the Cardinal's hand in this.

Anne He knows, I am sure of it.

Constant His spies are everywhere.

Anne Oh Constant! If only I had listened to you! I should never have given the wretched Quiche to dearest Totty! What am I to do?

Constant There is only one chance, Majesty. You must send an emissary to England bearing a letter to Tottenham. The Quiche must be brought back.

Anne By the day after tomorrow?! C'est impossible!

Constant Not if we act quickly.

Anne But who can I trust?

Constant There is one person, Your Majesty. A boy only, but with the heart of a lion. D'Artagnan is his name, and he is without.

Anne Oh dear, the poor love. (*She pauses*) Without what?

Constant I mean he's waiting outside.

Anne Oh. Then admit him.

Constant steps across to open the door and ushers D'Artagnan into the Queen's presence

D'Artagnan (*bowing*) Your Majesty.

Anne You are D'Artagnan?

D'Artagnan (*bowing again*) Yes, Your Majesty.

Anne Monsieur—I am undone.

D'Artagnan (*bowing and withdrawing*) I shall fetch safety pins, Majesty.

Anne You mistake me, Monsieur. I am sorely in need of a Knight errant.

D'Artagnan A Knight? But I'm just a pig farmer's boy.

Anne Under present circumstances, a pig farmer's boy errant will do.

D'Artagnan Do for what, Majesty?

Anne Do to perform a feat of supreme heroism, courage, and gallantry.

D'Artagnan Blimey!

Anne You will not undertake it, Monsieur?

D'Artagnan Er... This wouldn't happen to be an act calculated to make all France cry "Bravo!", would it?

Anne Potentially.

D'Artagnan Then I'm your man. Rest assured, Majesty. The True Quiche shall be made whole.

Act II, Scene 7

Anne C'est fantastique! (*To the audience*) I love it when a flan comes together...
Constant D'Artagnan—her Majesty will give you your instructions. I'll fetch pen and paper.

Lights down

Scene 7

The dungeon

The flickering firelight of the braziers reveals a Hellish scene straight from Dante's Inferno

Brothers Bastinado and Strappado, stripped to the waist and gleaming with sweat (but still wearing their pointy hoods) labour to load huge slabs of granite on to the chest of the recumbent Athos. As each slab is placed, Athos emits a mighty groan of inhuman agony. Eventually a bell tolls nearby, and the Inquisitors immediately cease their work, pick up their robes, and depart for prayer through the doorway L

Athos (*muffled through his iron mask*) Hey! Where are you two creeps going?! Got something more pressing on?! (*He manages to laugh weakly before subsiding back into groans*)

The door R creaks open and two more hooded figures enter

1st Figure Here he is!
Athos Porthos! Aramis! Is it you? Thank God! I knew you'd come.
1st Figure Please! Save your breath.
Athos Stuff that! Get this poxy chamberpot off my head and pass the cognac!
2nd Figure Stay calm. We'll have you out of here in a moment—when we've worked out how to shift these slabs of rock.
Athos Oh, don't worry about that. (*He sits up, flinging the pile of slabs off his chest*) It's only polystyrene.
1st Figure Keep still, mon ami, we'll soon have that mask off.

But just as they succeed in prising open the iron mask, two more red-robed and hooded figures leap into the dungeon through the doorway L

3rd Figure What are you doing?! Unhand him, you disciples of Satan!
1st Figure Stand back, you scarlet vulture! We are taking this man out of here.

4th Figure (*seizing Athos by the hands*) Ha! Over our dead bodies! This fellow is coming with us!
2nd Figure (*seizing Athos by the feet*) I'm afraid not, because you see—we are rescuing him!
3rd Figure Rescuing him?! But that's impossible!
2nd Figure Oh yes—and why is that?
3rd Figure (*pulling Athos towards him*) Because we are rescuing him!
Athos Er, excuse me...
1st Figure (*pulling Athos back towards him*) Oh, no, you're not.
Athos Hallo...
4th Figure (*pulling Athos back towards him*) Oh, yes, we are.
Athos Excuse me...
2nd Figure (*pulling Athos back towards him*) Look, we were here first!
Athos (*shouting*) WILL YOU ALL SHUT UP A MINUTE! (*To the newcomers*) You two—who are you?!

The third and fourth figures drag off their hoods

Porthos! Aramis! My sworn companions!
Porthos Well, who did you expect—the...
Athos (*interrupting*) DON'T say it!
Aramis Wait a minute! If we're us—then who are you?

The first and second figures pull off their hoods

Zach Zach Rebleur!
Zoot And Zoot A Lor!
Zach Once—spineless lackeys of the Cardinal...
Zoot Now—fearless citizen-mutineers of the committee for public safety!
Aramis The what?!
Zoot The committee for public safety. The revolution is here, citizen! We're waging war on a bankrupt system— (*he pulls Athos back towards him*) and we're starting by liberating this political prisoner.
Porthos Oh, no, you're not, (*he pulls Athos back towards him*) 'cos we're liberating him, see.
Aramis Yeah! So go and be revolting somewhere else!
Athos FOR GOD'S SAKE! JUST LET GO OF ME, THE LOT OF YOU!! (*To the audience*) Morbleu! Being rescued is worse than being racked!
Zoot Wait—someone's coming!
Porthos Sacré Fromage! It must be those dogs of the Inquisition!
Aramis Right, everybody—hats on! (*He grabs a lump of rock and holds it behind his back*)

Deepest apologies to the wardrobe department, but two more red-robed

Act II, Scene 8

and hooded figures enter the room through the doorway L! Now there are six of them

Greetings, brothers. Do you mind if I ask you a question?

Brother Bastinado and Brother Strappado silently exchange a glance. Brother Bastinado fractionally inclines his head

Thank you. What I'd like to know is—do your heads go all the way to the top of your hoods?

Brother Bastinado and Brother Strappado silently exchange another glance. This time, Brother Bastinado fractionally shakes his head

No? Oh, good... It won't hurt if I do this, then! (*He wallops Brother Bastinado on the head with the rock*)

A huge punch-up ensues, in which nobody can really see who the other is. Eventually, however, two of the red-robed figures end up being forcibly manhandled on to the mortuary slabs and strapped down. The other four step back and dust their hands. Porthos and Aramis whip off their hoods

Right! Come, Athos, let's get you out of here. (*To the others*) I suggest you two clowns take the other way out ... and make yourselves scarce!

The other two mime an exaggerated thumbs up, and perform a hasty comic exit R, whilst Porthos and Aramis, half carrying Athos, quickly slip out of the door L

Now only the two hooded figures on the slabs remain. There is a momentary pause as these two regard each other

Zoot What do we do now, Zach?
Zach Zoot. If we ever get out of this alive—I'm going to kill you.

Lights down

Scene 8

A room in the Louvre Palace

Richeleeugh and Louis are arguing. De Trivialle stands to one side

Richeleeugh It is a disgrace, Your Majesty! Musketeers—breaking into the Bastille, manhandling Inquisitors of the Holy Church, freeing dangerous prisoners.
Louis Oh, do be quiet, Wicheleeugh! If your wuffians had not washly appwehended one of our Musketeers in the first place, none of this would have happened.
Richeleeugh But Your Majesty...
Louis Enough! The subject is closed! We do not wish to discuss it further. Now, how fare the pweparations for our woyal ball.
Richeleeugh I think it true to say, Majesty, that my plans are nearly complete.
Louis Twiffic. Ah. Here comes the Queen.

Anne enters, with Constant in attendance

They both curtsey to the King

Anne Your Majesty.
Louis My Queen. You look pale, my dove. Is anything wrong?
Anne No, Louis. I feel a little unwell, that is all.
Richeleeugh (*with deep concern*) Have you sent out for anything, Majesty?
Anne Oh, yes, your eminence. (*Unable to resist it*) To England, in fact.
Constant Your Majesty!
Richeleeugh (*unfazed*) England! Well... That must be a most unique preparation.
Anne Oh, it is. It's a cure for a headache.
Richeleeugh Ah, I too have a cure for headache, Majesty. Albeit somewhat extreme, involving as it does, removal of the head.
Anne Let us hope it does not come to that.
Richeleeugh Hope springs eternal, your Majesty.

Bowing to Louis, Anne and Constant exit

Louis She's not herself, you know, Wicheleeugh.
Richeleeugh Ah, the weight of history bears heavily upon a young woman's shoulders, Majesty. After all, in two days time she will be called upon to bring forth the True Quiche of Lorraine.
Louis Hmmm... You know of no weason, we suppose, Cardinal, why her Majesty should not be in a position to do so?
Richeleeugh (*innocence personified*) No indeed, Majesty. None whatsoever.
Louis I see. Vewy well. (*He turns away*) De Twivialle, a word in your pwivate.

Louis and De Trivialle exit

Richeleeugh Ha ha ha ha!! The game's afoot, Roquefort! The hare is running!
Roquefort The Queen spoke of England, your eminence. She must have sent for the Quiche!
Richeleeugh Of course she has, Roquefort—she has no alternative. But I am one step ahead of her.
Roquefort Shall I to England, eminence? To intercept the agents of the Queen, and consign her portion of the Quiche to the wheelie-bin of history?
Richeleeugh No, Roquefort. Tomorrow, you must journey to the Carmelite Convent at Bèthune, to secure the King's portion of the Quiche, and convey it straightway to the ballroom of Versailles.
Roquefort But England, your eminence! The Duke of Tottenham!
Richeleeugh Forget Tottenham, Roquefort. That is already taken care of. You see, I have my best man on the job. Ha ha ha ha!!

Lights down

SCENE 9

London. The bedchamber of the Duke of Tottenham

A huge four-poster stands c, with an occasional table with decanter and glasses beside it

Panting and squeaking noises emanate from behind the drawn curtains of the bed. Muffled voices can also be heard

Tottenham Come on! Come on! That's the way! Keep tugging at it!
Malady But it's so stiff, Your Grace.
Tottenham Nearly there! One last heave!
Malady Finished!
Tottenham Ohhhh! What a relief!

The curtains swish back to reveal Tottenham sitting upon his bed, whilst Malady Du Splinter holds his boots

Thank you, Malady. Such a damnable struggle to get one's boots off.
Malady Lucky I stopped by, Your Grace.
Tottenham I should say! My manservant has just popped out.
Malady Yes. I noticed.
Tottenham Well, Malady—what a perfectly topping surprise! What brings you to London?

Malady Alas—Your Grace left Paris in such a hurry, we scarcely had time to bid adieu.
Tottenham How remiss of me. To fail to make my farewells to the most beautiful woman in all France.
Malady Surely, Your Grace, the Queen is the most beautiful woman in that happy country.
Tottenham Ah, but we're not in that happy country just now—are we?
Malady No indeed. Although I feel sure you must keep some fond memory of her Majesty close to your heart.
Tottenham Well, yes, I do have a certain keepsake—beneath me pillow, doncha know.
Malady How romantic—I should love to see it.
Tottenham (*smoothly*) Play your cards right, old girl, and perhaps you will.
Malady I understand you, Monsieur. How about a nightcap?
Tottenham No, thank you. Never wear one.
Malady (*pouting prettily*) Oh. But I have a flask of the finest Armangac. Surely Your Grace will not refuse to drink the health of the Queen of France?
Tottenham Ha! I should say not!
Malady Well, then... (*She pours two glasses of Armagnac, and hands one to Tottenham*)
Tottenham Thanks awfully. (*He raises his glass*) To Anne, the most beautiful woman in all France! (*He swallows his Armagnac*)
Malady To Anne—may her pretty head soon be separated from her lovely shoulders.
Tottenham (*shocked*) What?!
Malady Night night.
Tottenham Uuurggh! (*He keels over*)
Malady Ha ha ha ha ha!! Smooth as mayonnaise! (*She viciously kicks Tottenham's inert form. Hissing*) You vainglorious English muffin! (*Rummaging beneath his pillow, she pulls out the walnut-inlaid box*) Here's what I've come for... And the only tart in this bedchamber of any interest to me!

There is an abrupt hammering on a door below

D'Artagnan (*off*) Open the door! In the name of France!
Malady And not a moment too soon, if I'm not mistaken. Au revoir—Hotspur. Sleep well, Your Grace. We shall not meet again until the triumphant armies of France are tramping down Whitehall—and your noble head is rolling in a blood-soaked basket! Ha ha ha ha!!

Audience participation as Malady slips off R, *as D'Artagnan barges on* L

Act II, Scene 10

He races to the bed and shakes Tottenham

D'Artagnan Your Grace! Your Grace! Wake up!
Tottenham (*groggily*) Uhh? What? Eh? Who the devil are you, sir?
D'Artagnan D'Artagnan, Your Grace. I bear a letter from the Queen of France!
Tottenham God, my head...
D'Artagnan Here, read it.
Tottenham (*blearily*) What does she want?
D'Artagnan The Quiche, Your Grace. Her Majesty's life is in mortal peril!
Tottenham Good God! Then you must take it at once! Here, it's under the pillow. It's... (*He feels under his pillow*) Oh, cripes! It's gone!
D'Artagnan Gone?!
Tottenham Gone! Great Scott! Malady De Splinter—she was here earlier. The traitorous witch must have snaffled it!
D'Artagnan Morbleu! The she-devil!
Tottenham (*in despair*) My God—the Queen. She is lost!
D'Artagnan No, Your Grace! Not while D'Artagnan lives, breathes, and has a reckless gasp left in his body! I shall give chase to the wicked Malady, and relieve her of her precious burden.
Tottenham Pray God the hellcat hath not pitched it straightway into the Thames.
D'Artagnan No. She will straight to Richeleeugh. I must pursue her! Farewell, Your Grace!

D'Artagnan races out

Tottenham God speed, D'Artagnan! (*He stands unsteadily*) How could I have been so damnably foolish?! Me! The prime minister of England! I mean, it's not as though I'm stupid, is it? (*He shakes his head*) My God. I need a drink. (*He picks up Malady's untouched glass, and throws back the Armangac*) Uuuuurghh! (*He keels over on to the bed again*)

Lights down

SCENE 10

Paris. A street

Plonquer enters, leading Aramis, Porthos, Athos, and Constant

Porthos Are you sure about this, Plonquer?

Plonquer Course I'm sure. My young master—the reckless puppy—was popping across to England to bring back the Quiche, and said for you three gents and Madame H to meet him here.

D'Artagnan runs on

Aramis D'Artagnan!
Constant D'Artagnan! Thank God you are safe! You have the Quiche?!
D'Artagnan (*out of breath*) I'm afraid not. Malady de Splinter—she got there before me. Slipped Tottenham a Mickey Finn and made off with the Quiche. I dogged her track to Dover, crossed the Channel but an hour behind her, and rode like the wind to the gates of Paris. She can be no more than two minutes ahead of me. She's here somewhere! We must seek her out!
Constant Scour the streets, Messieurs! Find Malady! The Queen's life depends upon it!
Musketeers (*drawing their swords*) For the Queen!

They race off in different directions, leaving an empty stage

A moment later, Malady slips on

Malady Curse that lick-spittle Gascon poodle of the Queen! The tenacious wretch pursued me to the very gates of Paris. I know the mangy cur is somewhere close by—joined, no doubt, by those footloose fairy cakes, the Three Musketeers! (*She paces, muttering to herself*) But what to do? Try to slip through the streets to the Palais de Justice, and run the risk of being apprehended by the King's Musketeers? Non! I cannot be found with the Quiche upon my person. So... I must dispose of it here and now. But how? If I hide it, it is sure to be found. My God, but if only I had a prize sow to feed it to!

The Dame enters, crawling on her hands and knees

Dame Ooooh! Food! Please... Somebody throw me their scraps! I've been here three poxy days and I haven't eaten a thing!
Malady (*calling to her*) Hey, you—old mère!
Dame Who are you calling an old mare, you flossed-up filly!
Malady (*explaining*) Mère—it's French for mother.
Dame Oh. Right. Pardonnez-moi... Do go on.
Malady Are you hungry?
Dame No. I'm blinkin' ravenous!
Malady You poor poor thing. Here—why don't you eat this?

Dame What is it?
Malady It's quiche.
Dame Don't you want it?
Malady No. I've already eaten half. (*She opens the box*) See? Besides, I fancy your need is greater than mine.
Dame Oh, what a dear, sweet, considerate child. (*To the audience*) Isn't she a dear, sweet, considerate child, everybody?

Audience participation

Oh, yes, she is... A bit stuck-up, I grant you—but that's the Riviera set for you.
Malady (*losing patience*) Look, do you want it or don't you?
Dame All right! Keep your barnet buttoned. (*She peers into the box*) It's a bit green around the edges, isn't it?
Malady That's the asparagus.
Dame It seems to be glowing.
Malady Genetically modified asparagus.
Dame Oh. Right. Well— (*she takes the box*) ta very much, then.
Malady My pleasure. Bon appetit! Ha ha ha ha!!

Audience participation

Dame (*nodding towards the audience*) What's the matter with them, then?
Malady Who cares? They're English. Very small-minded people.

Audience participation

Dame (*to the audience*) Don't you think I should eat it, then?

Audience participation

Well, that's all right for you to say, isn't it? I mean, you lot have been out the back there, stuffing your greedy faces with mince pies and Mars bars!
Porthos (*off*) Hey! There she is! Seize that woman!
Malady I must fly! (*To the Dame*) Enjoy!

Malady flits off

Constant runs on

Constant STOP! Don't eat that!
Dame You're too late—it's mine. You're not having any!
Constant NO!!

But the Dame crams the whole thing into her mouth in a revolting display of gluttony

Dame (*spitting bits of quiche everywhere*) Yum! De-lish!

Constant snatches the walnut-inlaid box

D'Artagnan runs on

D'Artagnan Auntie!
Dame D'Artagnan! There you are, you little scamp! I've been looking for you all over Paris.
D'Artagnan (*numb with horror*) What have you done?!
Dame Well, I've done Nôtre Dame and the Champs Elysée—but I haven't done the Eiffel Tower because they haven't built it yet.
D'Artagnan (*stunned*) You ate the Quiche...
Dame Yes. I know... Gastronomic heresy. Ordinarily I wouldn't touch it. Waste of good eggs. Highly overrated, if you ask me. But—needs must.
D'Artagnan (*disbelieving*) She ate the Quiche...
Dame (*confiding*) Tell you the truth, I think it might have been a bit past its sell-by date.
D'Artagnan (*incredulously*) A bit?! (*Shouting*) It was over eight hundred years old!
Dame Oh. Not what you'd call nouvelle cuisine, then.
D'Artagnan Morbleu! My auntie's eaten the True Quiche of Lorraine. What are we going to do?
Plonquer There's only one thing we can do. Steal the other half.
Aramis Steal?
Porthos Steal?
Athos Steal?
Plonquer Well. Purloin then.
D'Artagnan Good idea. Let's go.
Porthos Wait! (*Sternly*) D'Artagnan... We are Musketeers of the King. The noblest swordsmen in all Europe. We cannot possibly sink to such tawdry pursuits as thievery.
D'Artagnan No. (*He nods to the Dame*) But she can.
Dame Eh?
D'Artagnan In fact, you could say "tawdry" is her middle name.
Dame Hang on a minute! Audrey is my middle name.
D'Artagnan But I could do with an escort, mes amis. Fellows I can trust.
Constant Please, Messieurs—I beg you. The Queen's life is in your hands.

The Three Musketeers exchange meaningful glances

Act II, Scene 11

Porthos Very well. We will undertake it.
Dame Oh, marvellous...
Constant (*relieved*) Thank you. I must to her Majesty. (*She touches D'Artagnan's hand*) Have a care, D'Artagnan...
D'Artagnan I shall. (*He glances at his comrades and smiles as he corrects himself*) We shall.
All (*shouting*) All for one, and one for all!

Song 7

Lights down

SCENE 11

Without the Carmelite Convent. A doorway

Aramis, Porthos, Athos and Plonquer enter

Porthos Right. Here we are. Go on, then—knock.

Plonquer knocks on the door

A nun answers

Nun What do you want?
Aramis This is the Carmelite Convent?
Nun It is.
Aramis Very well. Take me at once to the place where the Sixth Form girls are doing gym.
Porthos Aramis!
Aramis Sorry. Force of habit.
Porthos It's not that sort of convent! (*He takes over*) Good day to you, sister. You are mother superior?
Nun No, I am mother inferior.
Porthos (*nonplussed*) Oh. How so?
Nun I don't know. I'm just so worthless I suppose. I have a very low sense of self-esteem.
Porthos I see.
Nun The Cardinal says I am a waste of cloister space.
Athos For once, I'm inclined to agree with him.
Aramis (*hastily*) We have come to do veneration to the True Quiche of Lorraine. Will you admit us?

Nun No.
Aramis Why not?
Nun Because you're men. Men are not allowed. (*She bangs the door shut in their faces*)
Aramis Ah.
Athos Oh, well... That's that, then. (*Cheering up*) Everybody down the pub.
Porthos (*pulling him back*) Hold on! All right. Plan B. Plonquer—where is she?
Plonquer Just coming, sir.

The Dame and D'Artagnan enter, disguised as nuns

Dame I don't like this. Why do I get to wear the penguin suit?
D'Artagnan Because you're a woman. And we're all men.
Dame (*forgetting herself for a moment*) Are you?

D'Artagnan and the Musketeers strike butch poses

So you are.
D'Artagnan Thank you. (*He pushes the Dame forward*) Now get in there.
Dame What about you?
D'Artagnan Don't worry, I'll be right behind you.

The others hide as D'Artagnan knocks on the door

Dame But why do I have to do the talking?
D'Artagnan Look. Stop complaining. If it wasn't for you, we wouldn't be in this mess.

The nun answers the door again

Nun Yes?
Dame Hallo. I am Sister Mary Assumption.
Athos (*whispering loudly*) Hairy Consumption.
Porthos (*hissing*) Shut it.
Nun Indeed? From which convent, sister?
Dame Which convent? Oh... Er... St Michael.
Nun Ah. Would that be St Michael Hermit Penitent?
Dame No, dear. St Michael—Home Furnishings, Pricey.
Nun You are welcome, sister. Please come in.
Dame Ta ever so. We have come to do veneration to the True Quiche of Lorraine.
Nun Then you must make haste, sister, for we are expecting the Cardinal's representative to collect the relic at any moment.

Act II, Scene 11   71

Dame Well, we'd better get a wriggle on, then, hadn't we?
Nun Wait. Who is this?
Dame This? Oh, that's ... er... Sister Beaujolais Noveau.
Nun Noveau? She is a novice?
Dame Not yet. But give her time, and I'm sure she will be.
Nun Bless you, sister.

D'Artagnan inclines his head

Dame Oh. She's ... er ... taken a vow of silence.
Nun Why?
Dame Because her great big flapping gob kept getting her into trouble—didn't it, dear?

D'Artagnan glares at her

She says yes.
Nun I will show you to the chapel of the Sacred Quiche. This way...

The curtains open to reveal a chapel. An identical walnut-inlaid box stands on a small plinth, C, with a large cross of Lorraine on the wall behind. Another nun is just rising from prayer

This holy sister has also been paying her respects.
Dame Oh, that's nice.
2nd Nun (*falsetto*) Bless you, sisters.
Dame No, bless you, sister.
2nd Nun (*man's voice*) Suit yourself.

The Second Nun hurries out

Nun Well. I shall leave you alone to your devotions.
Dame How kind.

The First Nun goes out

D'Artagnan grabs the Dame

D'Artagnan Auntie! That nun! I'm sure I knew her.
Dame Of course you knew her. She just let us in.
D'Artagnan No. Not her. The other one. She seemed strangely familiar.
Dame The tension's getting to you—let's get on with the heist. (*She crosses to the box*) Here it is! Now what?

D'Artagnan Let me see! (*He examines the box*) Right—quickly! Mount a diversion!
Dame A diversion? What sort of diversion?
D'Artagnan I don't know... Tell a joke or something! (*He pulls a bag from beneath his robes and busies himself with the box*)
Dame Ah! A joke... Er... Right, then... (*She comes down to the audience*) I say, I say, I say! Did you hear the one about the nun that couldn't stop picking her nose? Do you know what her problem was?

Audience participation

That's right—she had a dirty habit!

Audience participation

A dirty habit, see! (*She explains*) Nun's robes are called habits—geddit? Picking your snitch is a dirty habit! IT'S A JOKE! Cor blimey! Go back to sleep. I'll give you a nudge when we've finished. (*To D'Artagnan*) Have you got it yet?
D'Artagnan Nearly!
Dame Well, hurry up! Someone's coming!
D'Artagnan What?!
Dame Someone's coming!
D'Artagnan Finished! (*He springs away from the plinth*)
Dame Too late!

Roquefort strides into the chamber

Eeeek! It's him! The Count of Lobster Thermidor!
Roquefort You! What are you doing here? You're supposed to be feeding the sticklebacks!
Dame Yes, well, that's where you're wrong! I've come for that!
Roquefort (*drawing his rapier*) You insolent pile of blubber! Stand away from that casket, or I'll spike your fat belly with more holes than a Swiss cheese! (*He seizes the box*) Fortunately for you I am in haste, else I would show you the price of meddling in the affairs of the Cardinal—but there will be another occasion, I am sure. Ha ha ha ha!!

Audience participation as Roquefort turns on his heel and strides from the chamber

Dame (*rounding on D'Artagnan*) Well, thank you so much, the Flashing Blade! What did you let him get away for?! Why didn't you dazzle him with your brilliant swordplay?!

Act II, Scene 12   73

D'Artagnan Because I've already got what we came for, that's why!
Dame Have you?! So what's laughing boy just whisked away in that box then?
D'Artagnan Wait and see! Come on! Let's get out of here!

The Dame and D'Artagnan exit

Lights down

Scene 12

Le maison de Monsieur Hoh-hi-hon

Hoh-hi-hon is on his way out

Hoh-hi-hon (*calling*) Gérard? Gérard?! Confound that snail! Where's he got to? Gérard, it's your big night, my beauty! Dinner at Versailles! His Majesty awaits! You don't want to keep the King waiting, do you?! Morbleu! Sometimes I think that snail has got more sense than I have! Oh, well, I'll just have to go without him.

Hoh-hi-hon goes out

A few moments later, the door creaks open again, and D'Artagnan and the Dame enter

Dame What are we doing back here?
D'Artagnan Look! Constant took the walnut-inlaid box. We need it. We can hardly turn up with the True Quiche in a Musketeer's hat, can we? The box must be here somewhere.
Dame I don't like this.
D'Artagnan Oh, stop panicking. Hoh-hi-hon's scuttled off to the ball, and Plonquer's keeping watch outside.
Dame So where's this precious box, then?
D'Artagnan Let me see. (*He looks round*) Aha! Over here. (*He seizes the box off a shelf—but cannot open it*) Merde! It's stuck! I can't get it open. Give me a hand, will you?
Dame What about the Quiche?
D'Artagnan Well, put it down for a moment.
Dame Put it down?! I can't just leave it on the floor, can I?
D'Artagnan Well, stick it in that cupboard then!
Dame Oh. Right. (*She opens the cupboard door*)

Gérard Drippy-Dew is hiding inside

Evening, Gérard... (*She slides the Quiche inside, and closes the door*)
D'Artagnan Right. Are you ready now?
Dame Fit as a flea.
D'Artagnan And twice as irritating. All right then. Pull!

Together they manage to prise the box open

Done it!
Dame Hooray!
D'Artagnan Auntie.
Dame Yes dear?
D'Artagnan Who's Gérard?
Dame Gérard Drippy-Dew? Why he's a great big enormous snail, that's all.
D'Artagnan (*repeating slowly*) A great big enormous snail.
Dame That's it.
D'Artagnan I see...

Pause

Auntie...
Dame Yes, dear?
D'Artagnan What do great big enormous snails eat?
Dame Eat? Oh, anything really... The more rotten the better, preferably.
D'Artagnan What, like—really old, festering scraps of food, you mean?
Dame Yes. That's the sort of thing.
D'Artagnan How old exactly?
Dame Oh, older the better I should think.

There is a pregnant pause. They stare at each other, then both rush screaming to the cupboard door

D'Artagnan ⎫
Dame ⎭ (*together*) Gérard!!

They fling open the door. Gérard regards them. The Quiche is nowhere to be seen

D'Artagnan No!

Gérard belches contentedly

Dame Too late! He's scoffed it!

Act II, Scene 13 75

D'Artagnan (*bitterly*) Oh, perfect!
Dame Well, would you credit it? The True Quiche of Lorraine—troughed by a giant snail!
D'Artagnan What's so unbelievable about that? After all, the rest of it was eaten by a greedy fat slug!
Dame (*hurt*) D'Artagnan! (*She pauses*) Now what are we going to do?
D'Artagnan There's not much we can do, is there?

Pause. D'Artagnan looks up, eyes gleaming

Except of course, to go to the King and tell the truth.
Dame The truth! What—you mean about the Queen and her extra-curricular activities?
D'Artagnan No! About you and Gérard Drippy-Dew hoovering up the most sacred gastronomic relic in all France!
Dame But you can't! We'd all be for the chop.
D'Artagnan Auntie. I am a D'Artagnan. I cannot fail Constant, and I will not fail the Queen. Now come—you and I have a dinner appointment at Versailles.

D'Artagnan drags the Dame off

Lights down

Scene 13

Versailles. The ballroom

A Major-domo announces the guests as they arrive

Major-domo His eminence, Cardinal Richeleeugh. Le Chevalier Du Lobster Roquefort. Malady De Splinter.

The trio of baddies walk downstage

Richeleeugh You have The Quiche, Roquefort?
Roquefort Yes, your eminence.
Richeleeugh (*gloating*) Then the night is ours.
Malady And at dawn, the Queen will keep an appointment in the execution yard of the Bastille. Ha ha ha ha!!

Audience participation as the baddies retire upstage to make way for...

Major-domo The King's Musketeers. Porthos, Athos, and Aramis.

The Three Musketeers enter, each striking a macho pose

Athos Where's the bar?
Aramis Where are the babes?
Porthos Where's the buffet?
Musketeers WOOF!
Major-domo Monsieur De Trivialle, Commandante of the King's Musketeers.
Athos Oh, no! Some party this is going to be!
De Trivialle (*spotting them*) You three wastrels!
Musketeers Oui, Mon Capitan!
De Trivialle Don't start that again. Just keep your wits about you. I'm expecting trouble.
Aramis (*aside*) You're telling us...

The Musketeers and De Trivialle retire upstage

Major-domo Monsieur Hubért Henri Hoh-hi-hon. Madame Hoh-hi-hon.
Hoh-hi-hon Do you think, my dear, that for just one evening you could refrain from meddling in Palace politics?

The Queen enters behind the King

Constant (*coldly*) Excusé-moi. I must speak with the Queen.
Hoh-hi-hon (*to the audience*) Obedient as ever. (*He shuffles gloomily off into a corner*)

Constant crosses to whisper to the Queen

Major-domo His most Catholic Majesty, Louis, by the grace of God, King of France.

Fanfare. Polite applause

Louis Gweetings, my loyal subjects. Welcome to our woyal wedding anniversawy ball.
Major-domo Her Majesty, Queen Anne.

Anne breaks off her whispered discussion with Constant, and comes downstage to join Louis, c

Act II, Scene 13   77

Louis Ah... Welcome, my Queen. Is aught amiss? Your cheek is deathly pale.
Anne I feel sick to the stomach, Majesty. (*She glances back at Constant*) I have just received ill news.
Richeleeugh Ah. Perchance your remedy from England has failed to arrive?
Anne (*coldly*) How could it arrive, your eminence, having been stolen?
Richeleeugh Dear me. Then we may have to employ my patent cure for headache after all.

D'Artagnan, the Dame, and Plonquer enter

Major-domo Monsieur D'Artagnan. Madame Desirée D'Artagnan.
Richeleeugh What the devil is that walrus doing here?!

The Major-domo is having trouble with Plonquer's name. After a moment's confusion he announces

Major-domo A plonker.

Plonquer remonstrates with the Major-domo, whilst D'Artagnan hurries donwstage to accost the King

D'Artagnan Your Majesty!
Louis Ah! D'Artagnan, n'est pas?
D'Artagnan Yes, Your Majesty.
Louis And who is this, er ... delightfully bucolic cweature?
Dame (*aside*) What's bucolic?
D'Artagnan My Auntie, Your Majesty. Desirée.
Dame (*aside*) Anyone know what bucolic means?
Louis Ah! Desirée... Enchanté.

Plonquer crosses to join the Dame

Dame Oh, I say! Likewise, your enormity. (*She turns to Plonquer*) I'm bucolic, I am...
Plonquer (*aside*) Bubonic...
D'Artagnan I must speak with you, Your Majesty. A matter of urgency.
Louis Later, my boy, later. Pleasure before business, you know.
D'Artagnan But Your Majesty——
Richeleeugh (*interrupting with a snarl*) Did you not hear His Majesty, you Gascon worm's turd?! (*To Louis*) We should proceed to the formalities without delay, Sire. Perhaps the Queen would care to bring forth her portion of the True Quiche of Lorraine?

Louis All in good time, Cardinal. First, please be so kind as to pwoduce that portion which you hold in our woyal name.
Richeleeugh But of course, Majesty. It is here. (*He calls*) Roquefort!
Roquefort Your eminence!
Richeleeugh Bring forth the aged relic.
Roquefort (*pointing to the Dame*) What—her?
Richeleeugh Not her! The Quiche!
Roquefort Oh, right. Sorry.

Roquefort comes forward bearing one of the walnut-inlaid boxes

Your eminence...
Richeleeugh The True Quiche of Lorraine, Majesty. (*With a flourish, he lifts the box lid*)

Louis peers inside

Louis (*dubiously*) Weally? It wather looks to me like pork scwatchings.
Richeleeugh WHAT?!! (*He seizes the box and stares at the contents*)
Louis Pork scwatchings, Wicheleeugh... Cwispy fwied extwemities of piggy.
Richeleeugh (*thunderstruck*) But I don't understand... (*He rounds on Roquefort*) Roquefort!

Roquefort shrugs helplessly

Louis Oh deawie me.
Richeleeugh There has obviously been a misunderstanding, Majesty. Easily resolved, I have no doubt. Meanwhile, may I suggest we ask the Queen—where is her portion of the Quiche?!
Louis Her Majesty is about to produce it.
Richeleeugh (*through gritted teeth*) How can she produce it when she does not have it?
Louis Does not have it, siwwah? What makes you think so?
Richeleeugh (*shouting*) Because she gave it to her ridiculous English stud-muffin, that's why!
Louis Her stud-muffin?!
Richeleeugh The time for pretence is over, Your Majesty! The Queen gave France's sacred relic to her secret lover—the Duke of Tottenham! (*He points the finger*) J'accuse! Let her deny it if she can!
Anne I...
Louis (*mildly*) Au contraire, Wicheleeugh. The Queen's portion of the Quiche is right here, is it not, my dove?

Act II, Scene 13   79

Anne Er... I...
Louis Of course it is. Monsieur De Twivialle has been holding it in safekeeping for you—dost wemember?
Anne Oh, yes.
Louis And here it is. (*To De Trivialle*) If you please, De Twivialle.
De Trivialle Your Majesty. (*He steps forward, bearing a plain wooden box*) Behold—The True Quiche of Lorraine! (*He opens the box*)

The faint green glow emanates from within, and distant sepulchral chords are heard

Richeleeugh (*white-faced*) Merde!
Dame (*aside*) Hang on a minute! How can that be the Quiche? Gérard ate it.
D'Artagnan (*aside*) No! Don't you see?! Somebody had already switched the Quiche before we got to the Carmelite convent. We never stole the True Quiche at all. Gérard ate a fake!
Dame Then we're off the hook?! Bonza!
Louis (*thoughtfully*) So, Cardinal. Her Majesty has produced her portion of the Quiche—but it seems that you are unable to produce mine.
Richeleeugh Majesty. There is obviously a perfectly sensible explanation.
Louis We are sure there is—but alas, you know the penalty for failure to produce the Quiche.
Richeleeugh Your Majesty, I beg you—let us not be hasty.
Louis Now, now, Cardinal! Wules are wules. (*He claps his hands*)

The brothers of the Inquisition enter, bearing the iron mask

We believe you are acquainted wiv Bwother Bastinado and Bwother Stwappado.
Richeleeugh No!
Louis Gweetings, bwothers. I fear we have a sinner in need of your stwict ministwations.
Richeleeugh No! Not the iron mask!
Louis Step forward, Cardinal Sin.

The Inquisitors lay hold of Richeleeugh

Richeleeugh No! How dare you lay your filthy hands on me?! Do you know who I am?! I am Richeleeugh! Cardinal of France! You have no jurisdiction over me. Who invited you to poke your nose in? I didn't ask you to come to Paris!

Pause

Louis No, I did.
Richeleeugh What?!
Louis Cardinal, you are the weakest link—goodbye.
Richeleeugh Nooooo!

The mask is lowered on to Richeleeugh's head. Again, there is an audible click as it is snapped shut, and his scream abruptly cut off

Louis To the Bastille with him.

Audience participation as the man in the iron mask is dragged out by the Inquisitors

Louis turns to regard Malady and Roquefort

    Malady De Splinter...
Malady Your Majesty!
Louis Le Chevalier Du Lobster Woquefort...
Roquefort Your Majesty!
Louis Your loyalty to the Cardinal does you credit.
Malady ⎫
Roquefort ⎭ (*together*) Thank you, Your Majesty.
Louis Your disloyalty to our own woyal personage, does not.
Malady (*throwing herself to the floor*) Mercy, Majesty! Mercy! Take pity on a poor, weak, defenceless female! I'll do anything you ask of me! Anything!
Roquefort And so will I!
Louis Very well... We want you both to get mawwied.
Malady (*puzzled*) Is that all?
Louis To each other.
Roquefort ⎫
Malady ⎭ (*together*) NO!!
Louis Further, we hereby appoint you joint Governors to our newly acquired dominion of The Unfortunate Islands in the French Equatorial Indies.
Roquefort (*surprised*) Thank you, Your Majesty.
Louis It's a collection of sun-scorched volcanic wocks, populated entirely by scorpions and poisonous snakes—so you should get on well with your new subjects. Your ship leaves tonight. Take them away.
Malady No!

Roquefort and Malady are dragged out

Louis turns to Queen Anne

Act II, Scene 13   81

Louis (*sternly*) Now, Madame.
Anne Oh, Louis... Please. Let me explain...
Louis Tush! We have long suspected that Wicheleeugh plotted to undermine our soveweign power. That is why we sent for agents of the Holy Inquisition. To keep watch on him. We were especially perturbed at his sudden, stwange insistence that you should pwoduce your portion of the True Quiche of Lowwaine.
Anne Louis, I...
Louis So, we wequested our dear comwade, Monsieur De Twivialle, to ensure that at least one half of the wetched thing would be on hand to save your bacon—should the need awise.
D'Artagnan (*aside, to De Trivialle*) It was you! Dressed as a nun!
De Trivialle (*aside*) And you, I believe. Also dressed as a nun.
D'Artagnan (*looking straight ahead*) I propose that we never mention it again.
De Trivialle (*looking straight ahead*) Agreed.
Louis We do not wish to know pwecisely how the dependable De Twivialle accomplished this task. Nor Madame, how you came to ... mislay your portion of the Twue Quiche of Lowwaine—if indeed you did. Suffice to say, that we expect your conduct in future to be beyond wepwoach, and your fidelity to the King of Fwance to be absolute.
Anne (*chastened*) Oh, Louis.
Louis (*softening*) And now—as this is our anniversary after all—we feel moved to gwant our dear wifelet a wequest. Ask anything in a King's power, my dove, and it shall be yours.
Anne Louis. For myself, I can ask no greater gift than the leniency and compassion you have already shown. Except perhaps, one day, your forgiveness. But for my dear, loyal friend, Constant Hoh-hi-hon, and her ardent admirer, D'Artagnan, I ask the following: make her a free woman, that she may wed the man she loves.
Louis Gladly. (*To Hoh-hi-hon*) Monsieur Hoh-hi-hon, it seems we must relieve you of your wife. How say you, Monsieur?
Hoh-hi-hon Go ahead. Relieve me. (*Aside*) That's more than she ever did. (*To Louis*) I say—good riddance, Majesty! I get more understanding from my snails.
Louis Vewy well. (*To Queen Anne*) And the Gascon?
Anne Oh Louis. Make him a Musketeer.
Louis A Musketeer? (*He frowns*) Has he then completed a feat of supweme hewoism, couwage, and gallantwy, calculated to make all Fwance cry "Bwavo!"?
Anne He has, Your Majesty.
Louis What was it, then?
Anne Please, Louis. Don't ask.

Louis I see... De Twivialle?
De Trivialle I concur, Majesty. With all my heart.
Louis In that case—approach, D'Artagnan.

D'Artagnan approaches and drops on to one knee before Louis

We understand your sword is broken, Monsieur ... that you have no sword?
D'Artagnan (*ashamed*) That is so, Your Majesty.
Louis (*gently*) Non, Monsieur. That is not so. (*He draws his own sword and hands it hilt first to D'Artagnan*) This is your sword.
D'Artagnan (*stunned*) But Majesty, that is your sword!
Louis D'Artagnan. This same vile Woquefort bwoke your father's twusty sword. Now, Fwance is your father and your mother. And Fwance's sword is your sword. Awise, D'Artagnan of Gascony, gentleman of the King's Musketeers.
D'Artagnan Your Majesty, I... I don't know what to say.
Dame Well, that's a first.
Louis How about: "All For One, and—" whatever the rest of it is.
D'Artagnan & Musketeers ALL FOR ONE, AND ONE FOR ALL! (*They slap their thighs*)
Louis That's the spiwit! (*He turns to De Trivialle*) I don't know, De Twivialle. They really are a bunch of old slappers.
De Trivialle They certainly are, Majesty. (*He smiles*) They certainly are.

D'Artagnan sweeps Constant up in his arms

D'Artagnan Oh Constant! Quickly! The kiss of life!
Constant (*alarmed*) You are in shock, my love?
D'Artagnan No, I'm drowning in your eyes. Kiss me!

They kiss

Louis Ah... Young love. (*To De Trivialle*) Such a pity that the Quiche will never now be re-united. Still, it's only a mouldy old egg flan after all, and I've never been one for mumbo-jumbo.
De Trivialle To whom will Your Majesty turn for advice, now that Richeleeugh has been consigned to the Bastille?
Louis Oh, I've already appointed new ministers. (*To the Major-domo*) Ask the council of state to join us, will you?
Major-domo Call the Council of State!
Louis After the subterfuge of Cardinals and Queens, we felt a little down to earth advice might not go amiss.

Act II, Scene 13   83

Dame Oh, no… You haven't…
Louis We found these two engaging wascals slopping out the lower toilets of the Palais de Justice.
Dame You have…
Louis And you can't get much more down to earth than that—can you?
Major-domo (*announcing*) The Council of State to The King of France.

Zoot and Zach enter, now wearing ermine trimmed robes

Zoot Zoot A Lor!
Zach And Zach Rebleur!
Zoot ⎫ (*together*) Reporting for duty, your Munificence!
Zach ⎭
Dame But they're a couple of prize pillocks!
Louis Pwecisely. We have decided the safest course is to employ advisers who are profoundly more stupid than one's self.
Dame (*to Zoot and Zach*) Well, well—promoted from Cardinal's lapdogs to King's lackeys, eh? What happened to the revolution, then?
Zoot Well, you can't hurry history.
Zach That's right. Kings have got a bright future in France, you know!
Dame (*aside*) That's what you think! But hang on a minute. It's all right for you lot, gadding round Gay Paree in your happy ending—but where does all this leave me?! Back on the perishin' pig farm, I s'pose.
Hoh-hi-hon Not necessarily.
Dame Eh?
Hoh-hi-hon Well, cherie, it looks like I'm a free man. (*Lasciviously*) So how d'you fancy coming to live with me, eh?
Dame To be honest, I'd rather live in a ditch and eat compost.
Hoh-hi-hon (*rubbing his hands in delight*) Ooooh! Spoken like a true snail!
Dame Oh Gawd!
Zoot That's right. Tell the hideous Hubèrt where to stuff his escargots! You stick with Zoot and Zach—we know how to show an old bat a good time!
Zach Too right! How'd you fancy a *ménage a trois*?
Dame Well, let's just say I think I can *ménage* without you two berks.
Plonquer Here! What about me? I could do with a firm hand to keep me on the straight and narrow.
Dame You! Ha! Don't make me laugh! Your mitts are stickier than a bucket of profiteroles! I'd be forever looking out for me loose change!
Plonquer Picky, picky, picky!
D'Artagnan You see, Auntie—you have no end of suitors.
Dame Yes! Suitors that don't suit her! Look at 'em! What a bunch of no hope bin-ends.
De Trivialle Come, Madame. I need a housekeeper and perhaps a companion.

Dame Ooooh! Now you're talking! Companion to the Commandante of the King's Musketeers! (*To the audience*) That sounds a bit more like it, doesn't it, ladies?!
De Trivialle Well, Commandante of the King's Musketeers for the time being. I'm due to retire next year.
Dame Retire? What—to a life of leisure? Corking! Where are we off to, then? Monaco? St Tropez? Biarritz?
De Trivialle Well, do you know, I have a hankering to hang up my sword in my native Gascony.
Dame (*suspiciously*) Gascony?
De Trivialle Yes... I thought I might set myself up in a nice little pig farm.
Dame A pig farm in Gascony?! Oh, ruddy mervielleuse!
Louis Well. That's settled then. Now, we would like to end by pwoposing a Fwench toast. To gentlemen and ladies, principal boys and principal girls, stout-hearted Englishmen and gallant Fwenchmen evewywhere. (*He raises his glass*) Vive La Difference!
All Vive La Difference! Hooray!

Song 8

CURTAIN

Walkdown in the following order

1. *Wenches, innkeepers, etc.*
2. *Pus-sac and the Cardinal's Guard*
3. *Inquisitors and Mother Inferior*
4. *De Trivialle, Plonquer, Hoh-hi-hon*
5. *Louis, Anne, Tottenham*
6. *Roquefort, Malady, Richeleeugh*
7. *Zoot, Zach, and the Dame*
8. *Athos, Porthos, and Aramis*
9. *D'Artagnan and Constant*

LE R'APPROCHEMENT

Porthos	And so our classic tale concludes.
Athos	Our swashbuckling now is ended.
Aramis	We hope that you were all amused...
Dame	And if not amused—offended!
Constant	The moral is that valiant heart will always win fair hand.
Anne	And if you meet with wickedness—then you must make a stand.

Act II, Scene 13

Malady	And evil villains everywhere—note this down in your book:
Richeleeugh	That foolish Kings aren't always quite as stupid as they look!
Roquefort	All right! I think that's quite enough of this pointless rhyme...
Dame	It would be nice to reach the pub before they ring for time!
Louis	But if, like us, you've had a ball,
D'Artagnan	Shout "All For One, and One For All!"
Company	ALL FOR ONE, AND ONE FOR ALL!!

Chanson

CURTAIN

Bar-Tabac

FINIS

FURNITURE AND PROPERTY LIST

Further dressing may be added at the director's discretion

ACT I

Scene 1

On stage: Red throne
Red dais

Personal: **Roquefort:** rapier (worn throughout)

Scene 2

On stage: Trapdoor
Tavern table

Personal: **Wench:** notepad, pencil
Musketeers: swords (worn throughout)
Louis: sword (worn throughout)

Scene 3

On stage: Shovel

Scene 4

On stage: Table

Personal: **D'Artagnan:** glove, sword in scabbard (worn throughout)
Roquefort: cosh

Scene 5

On stage: Red throne
Red dais

Furniture and Property List

Scene 6

On stage: Table
Chairs
Plate with food

Personal: **Athos:** bottle of drink
Porthos: napkin

Scene 7

On stage: Large pink ear

Off stage: Large snail containing large wobbly ball of jelly (**SM**)

Scene 8

On stage: Bar
Cloth
Huge covered basket containing French breadsticks

Scene 9

Strike: Bar
Cloth
French breadsticks

Scene 10

On stage: Occasional table

Off stage: Small wooden box (**Constant**)

Personal: **Anne:** handkerchief

Scene 11

Strike: Occasional table

Off stage: Cloak, wheel-lock pistol (**Roquefort**)

ACT II

Scene 1

On stage: Mortuary-style slabs with straps
Box of implements
Pantomime scissors
Spider glove puppet
Shovel
Rubber Bart Simpson mask

Off stage: Huge, bright green, furry spider (**SM**)
Hideous iron mask (**Inquisitor**)

Personal: **Zach:** box of matches

Scene 2

On stage: Red throne
Red dais

Scene 3

Strike: Red throne
Red dais

Scene 4

On stage: As before

Scene 5

On stage: As before

Scene 6

On stage: Occasional table

Scene 7

On stage: Mortuary slabs
Huge slabs of granite
Lump of rock
Inquisitors' robes

Furniture and Property List

Personal: **Athos:** iron mask

Scene 8

Strike: Mortuary slabs
Slabs of granite
Lump of rock

Scene 9

On stage: Huge four-poster bed with curtains
Occasional table with decanter, glasses, bottle of Armagnac
Walnut-inlaid box

Scene 10

Strike: Bed
Occasional table

Off stage: Walnut-inlaid box (**Malady**)

Scene 11

On stage: Chapel
Small plinth. *On it*: walnut-inlaid box stands
Large cross of Lorraine

Personal: **D'Artagnan:** bag

Scene 12

On stage: Shelf. *On it*: box
Large pantomime snail

Scene 13

Strike: Shelf

Off stage: Walnut-inlaid boxes (**Roquefort**)
Plain wooden box (**De Trivialle**)
Iron mask (**Inquisitors**)

LIGHTING PLOT

Property fittings required: nil
Various interior and exterior settings

ACT I, Scene 1

To open: Shaft of light through cruciform, slit window

Cue 1   **Richeleeugh** laughs   (Page 2)
          Lights down

ACT I, Scene 2

To open: Lights up on forestage

Cue 2   **Plonquer**: "And a frustrated Musketeer."   (Page 9)
          Crossfade to next scene

ACT I, Scene 3

To open: Sunshine

Cue 3   Jaunty French music starts up   (Page 11)
          Lights down

ACT I, Scene 4

To open: Overall general lighting

Cue 4   **Zach & Zoot**: "He's going to start to smell…"   (Page 15)
          Lights down

Lighting Plot

ACT I, SCENE 5

To open: Overall general lighting

No cues

ACT I, SCENE 6

To open: Overall general lighting

Cue 5	**Athos**: "Nutter…" *Lights down, then up on another part of the stage*	(Page 18)
Cue 6	**D'Artagnan** dashes off *Lights down, then up on another part of the stage*	(Page 19)
Cue 7	**D'Artagnan**: "I think that all went rather well." *Black-out*	(Page 20)

ACT I, SCENE 7

To open: Overall general lighting

Cue 8	The **Dame** and **Hoh-hi-hon** exit *Lights down*	(Page 23)

ACT I, SCENE 8

To open: Overall general lighting

Cue 9	**Athos**: "It'll never catch on." *Black-out*	(Page 28)

ACT I, SCENE 9

To open: Overall general lighting

Cue 10	**D'Artagnan** and **Plonquer** shake hands *Lights down*	(Page 31)

ACT I, Scene 10

To open: Overall general lighting

Cue 11 **Anne** opens box (Page 33)
Faint green glow in box

Cue 12 Music abates (Page 34)
Lights down

ACT I, Scene 11

To open: Overall general lighting

Cue 13 After Song 4 (Page 40)
Lights down

ACT II, Scene 1

To open: Overall general lighting

Cue 14 **Athos**'s scream suddenly cuts off (Page 48)
Black-out

ACT II, Scene 2

To open: Overall general lighting

Cue 15 Audience participation after **Richeleeugh** laughs (Page 51)
Lights down

ACT II, Scene 3

To open: Overall general lighting

Cue 16 **Zach** and **Zoot** exit (Page 53)
Lights down

Lighting Plot

ACT II, Scene 4

To open: Overall general lighting

Cue 17   **Hoh-hi-hon** exits, chuckling   (Page 56)
           Lights down then straight up on next scene

ACT II, Scene 5

To open: Overall general lighting

No cues

ACT II, Scene 6

To open: Overall general lighting

Cue 18   **Constant**: "I'll fetch pen and paper."   (Page 59)
           Lights down

ACT II, Scene 7

To open: Flickering firelight

Cue 19   **Zach**: "...I'm going to kill you."   (Page 61)
           Lights down

ACT II, Scene 8

To open: Overall general lighting

Cue 20   **Richeleeugh** laughs   (Page 63)
           Lights down

ACT II, Scene 9

To open: Overall general lighting

Cue 21   **Tottenham** keels over (Page 65)
           Lights down

ACT II, Scene 10

To open: Overall general lighting

Cue 22   After Song 7 (Page 69)
           Lights down

ACT II, Scene 11

To open: Overall general lighting

Cue 23   The **Dame** and **D'Artagnan** exit (Page 73)
           Lights down

ACT II, Scene 12

To open: Overall general lighting

Cue 24   **D'Artagnan** drags the **Dame** off (Page 75)
           Lights down

ACT II, Scene 13

To open: Overall general lighting

Cue 25   **De Trivialle** opens box (Page 79)
           Faint green glow from box

EFFECTS PLOT

ACT I

No cues

ACT II

Cue 2   **Inquisitors** load slabs of granite on **Athos**   (Page 59)
Bell tolls nearby

www.ingramcontent.com/pod-product-compliance
Ingram Content Group UK Ltd.
Pitfield, Milton Keynes, MK11 3LW, UK
UKHW021843210426
5322IPUK00022B/443